SpringerBriefs in Psychology

SpringerBriefs present concise summaries of cutting-edge research and practical applications across a wide spectrum of fields. Featuring compact volumes of 55 to 125 pages, the series covers a range of content from professional to academic. Typical topics might include:

- A timely report of state-of-the-art analytical techniques
- A bridge between new research results as published in journal articles and a contextual literature review
- A snapshot of a hot or emerging topic
- An in-depth case study or clinical example
- A presentation of core concepts that readers must understand to make independent contributions

SpringerBriefs in Psychology showcase emerging theory, empirical research, and practical application in a wide variety of topics in psychology and related fields. Briefs are characterized by fast, global electronic dissemination, standard publishing contracts, standardized manuscript preparation and formatting guidelines, and expedited production schedules.

Federico Addimando

Client-Centered Business Consulting

The Power of Psychological Understanding

 Springer

Federico Addimando
Contributor at China Media Group
CEO - MF International
Shanghai, China

ISSN 2192-8363   ISSN 2192-8371   (electronic)
SpringerBriefs in Psychology
ISBN 978-3-031-42843-2   ISBN 978-3-031-42844-9   (eBook)
https://doi.org/10.1007/978-3-031-42844-9

This Springer imprint is published by the registered company Springer Nature Switzerland AG
The registered company address is: Gewerbestrasse 11, 6330 Cham, Switzerland

Paper in this product is recyclable.

Introduction

Business consulting is a complex field that requires a deep understanding of human psychology, organizational behavior, and business processes. Successful consultants need to be able to build strong relationships with their clients, communicate effectively, and provide customized solutions that drive tangible results. In this book, we explore the psychology behind effective business consulting. We dive into the various factors that shape client behavior and decision-making, and we provide insights into the most effective techniques and strategies for building rapport, establishing trust, and delivering value.

We cover a range of topics, from the initial client engagement to the final deliverable, and we provide real-world examples and case studies to illustrate the concepts we discuss. We also address common challenges and obstacles that consultants face, and we provide practical guidance on how to overcome them. Whether you are a seasoned consultant looking to refine your skills or a new consultant seeking to build a solid foundation, this book is designed to provide you with the tools and knowledge you need to succeed in the dynamic and demanding world of business consulting.

Contents

Chapter 1
Becoming a Business Consultant

Consulting is a highly sought-after profession that requires a combination of skills, knowledge, and experience. Whether you're just starting your career or considering a career change, becoming a business consultant can be a rewarding and fulfilling path. In this chapter, we will discuss the steps you can take to become a business consultant, starting with choosing the right educational path.

When it comes to choosing the right educational path, there are a lot of factors to consider. It can be overwhelming and confusing, but it's important to take the time to carefully weigh your options and make an informed decision. As someone who has gone through this process myself, I can offer some personal considerations to keep in mind.

First and foremost, it's important to think about your career goals. What kind of consulting do you want to specialize in? Are you interested in management consulting, financial consulting, or perhaps technology consulting? Each of these fields requires a different set of skills and knowledge, so it's important to choose an educational path that aligns with your career aspirations.

In my own experience, I was drawn to management consulting. I wanted to help organizations improve their operations and strategy, so I knew that I needed a solid foundation in business and management. This led me to pursue a Bachelor's degree in Business Administration with a specialization in Management. However, your own career goals may differ, so it's important to take the time to reflect on what you want to achieve in your consulting career.

Another important consideration is your personal interests. As I went through my own educational journey, I discovered that I was particularly interested in topics such as leadership, organizational behavior, and strategy. Choosing a program that aligned with my interests made my educational experience more enjoyable and fulfilling. It also helped me stand out in a competitive job market, as I was able to demonstrate a genuine passion for my work.

Of course, budget is also an important consideration when choosing an educational path. Pursuing a degree or certification can be expensive, so it's important to

© The Author(s), under exclusive license to Springer Nature Switzerland AG 2023
F. Addimando, *Client-Centered Business Consulting*, SpringerBriefs in
Psychology, https://doi.org/10.1007/978-3-031-42844-9_1

think about the costs involved. This may involve researching scholarships or other financial aid options, or considering a program that is more affordable but still meets your needs.

In addition to these personal considerations, there are other factors to keep in mind. For example, it's important to consider the reputation of the educational institution or program you are considering. Look for programs that are accredited and have a strong reputation within the industry. You can also research the employment outcomes for graduates of the program, which can give you a sense of the value of the degree or certification.

Another important factor to consider is practical experience. While formal education is important, practical experience is essential in the field of consulting. Look for programs that offer opportunities for hands-on learning, such as internships or project-based coursework. This can give you a competitive edge when applying for consulting jobs, as it demonstrates that you have real-world skills that can be applied in the workplace.

Finally, it's important to keep in mind that continuing education is essential in the field of consulting. New technologies, industry trends, and best practices are constantly emerging, and it's important to stay up-to-date on these developments. Look for programs that offer opportunities for continuing education, such as professional development courses, seminars, and conferences.

In conclusion, choosing the right educational path requires careful consideration of your career goals, personal interests, budget, and other factors. By reflecting on your own needs and doing your research, you can make an informed decision that will set you up for success in the field of business consulting.

1.1 Choosing the Right Educational Path

When it comes to becoming a business consultant, there are many different educational paths you can take. While a formal degree may not be required, having a solid educational foundation can give you an edge in the field. Here are some educational paths to consider:

- Business administration degree: A degree in business administration can provide you with a comprehensive understanding of business operations, management, marketing, and finance. This degree program typically covers a broad range of topics and prepares you for a variety of business-related careers, including consulting. It's important to note that a business administration degree may not be necessary, but it can help you stand out in a competitive job market.
- MBA: A Master of Business Administration (MBA) is a popular choice for those looking to become business consultants. This advanced degree program typically covers topics such as leadership, strategic planning, finance, and marketing. An MBA can provide you with a deeper understanding of business operations and prepare you for higher-level consulting roles. However, an MBA can be expensive

and time-consuming, so it's important to weigh the cost and benefits before pursuing this degree.

- Specialized degrees: There are also specialized degrees that can prepare you for specific consulting roles, such as a degree in accounting, finance, or marketing. These degrees can provide you with a deeper understanding of a particular aspect of business and can be helpful if you're interested in specializing in a specific area of consulting.
- Certifications: In addition to a degree, many consulting firms require or prefer certifications. These certifications can demonstrate your expertise in a particular area and can help you stand out in a competitive job market. Examples of certifications include Certified Management Consultant (CMC), Project Management Professional (PMP), and Certified Public Accountant (CPA).

It's important to research the educational requirements for the type of consulting you're interested in pursuing. Some consulting roles may require a specific degree or certification, while others may prioritize practical experience. Additionally, keep in mind that consulting is a field where continuous learning is essential, so be open to continuing education opportunities throughout your career.

In addition to formal education, there are other ways to gain knowledge and skills that can prepare you for a career in consulting. Consider attending seminars, workshops, and conferences in your area of interest. Networking with other professionals in the field can also provide you with valuable insights and connections.

Choosing the right educational path is just the first step in becoming a successful business consultant. In the following sections, we will discuss the importance of practical experience, building your personal brand, creating a network of contacts, and the role of certifications in consulting. By combining a solid educational foundation with practical experience and a strong professional network, you can set yourself up for success in the field of business consulting.

- Career goals: One of the first considerations to make when choosing an educational path is your career goals. What type of consulting do you want to specialize in? What level of education and experience is required for that role? Are you looking to work for a large consulting firm or start your own consulting business? Answering these questions can help you determine which educational path will best prepare you for your desired career path.
- Interests: Another important consideration is your interests. What subjects and topics are you passionate about? What type of consulting work do you enjoy doing? Choosing a degree or certification program that aligns with your interests can make your educational experience more enjoyable and fulfilling. It can also help you stand out in a competitive job market.
- Budget: Education can be expensive, so it's important to consider your budget when choosing an educational path. Can you afford to pursue a degree program or certification? Are there financial aid options available to you? Consider the cost of tuition, textbooks, and other related expenses when making your decision.
- Reputation: It's also important to consider the reputation of the educational institution or program you're considering. Is the program accredited? What is the

reputation of the faculty and staff? What are the employment outcomes for graduates of the program? These factors can help you determine the quality of education you'll receive and the value of the degree or certification.

- Practical experience: While formal education is important, practical experience is also essential in the field of consulting. Look for educational programs that offer opportunities for hands-on learning, such as internships, co-op programs, or project-based coursework. This can give you a competitive edge when applying for consulting jobs and help you develop real-world skills that can be applied in the workplace.
- Certifications: In addition to formal education, certifications can be valuable in the field of consulting. They demonstrate a level of expertise in a specific area and can help you stand out in a competitive job market. Research the certifications that are most relevant to your desired consulting field and determine the requirements for obtaining them.
- Continuing education: Finally, keep in mind that continuing education is essential in the field of consulting. New technologies, industry trends, and best practices are constantly emerging, and it's important to stay up-to-date on these developments. Look for educational programs that offer opportunities for continuing education, such as professional development courses, seminars, and conferences.
- Choosing the right educational path requires careful consideration of your career goals, interests, budget, and other factors. By researching your options, assessing your needs, and setting clear goals, you can make an informed decision about which educational path will best prepare you for a successful career in business consulting.

1.2   The Importance of Practical Experience

As someone who has worked in the field of business consulting for several years, I can attest to the importance of practical experience. While formal education is important, it can only take you so far. Practical experience is essential for developing the skills and knowledge needed to succeed in the field of consulting.

One of the key benefits of practical experience is that it allows you to apply the theories and concepts learned in the classroom to real-world situations. It's one thing to understand a particular business model or management theory in theory, but it's another thing entirely to see how it plays out in practice. Through practical experience, you can gain a deeper understanding of how businesses operate and how to apply your knowledge to solve real-world problems.

Another important benefit of practical experience is that it allows you to develop important skills such as critical thinking, problem-solving, and communication. In the field of consulting, these skills are essential. Clients come to consultants because they need help solving complex problems or improving their operations, and it's up to the consultant to provide solutions. By working on real-world projects, you can develop your ability to think critically, identify problems, and communicate effectively with clients.

Practical experience also allows you to develop a deeper understanding of the industry and the specific challenges facing businesses. No two businesses are exactly alike, and each industry has its own unique characteristics and challenges. By working on real-world projects, you can gain a better understanding of these factors and how they impact the work you do as a consultant.

Another benefit of practical experience is that it can help you build your professional network. Consulting is a relationship-based business, and the relationships you build with clients, colleagues, and industry leaders can be invaluable to your career. By working on projects with a variety of clients and colleagues, you can build relationships that can help you advance your career and open up new opportunities.

Of course, practical experience is not without its challenges. Consulting projects can be complex and demanding, and they often require you to work under tight deadlines and deal with difficult clients. However, these challenges can also be opportunities for growth and development. By overcoming these challenges, you can build your resilience and develop the skills needed to succeed in a fast-paced and dynamic industry.

The importance of practical experience cannot be overstated. While formal education is important, practical experience is essential for developing the skills and knowledge needed to succeed in the field of consulting. By working on real-world projects, you can gain a deeper understanding of the industry, develop important skills, and build your professional network. While practical experience can be challenging at times, the benefits far outweigh the costs.

When it comes to building a successful career in business consulting, formal education is certainly important, but practical experience is equally if not more essential. Practical experience provides you with the opportunity to apply what you've learned in the classroom to real-world situations, and develop the skills and knowledge needed to succeed as a consultant. Here are some key considerations to keep in mind when it comes to the importance of practical experience:

1.2.1   Application of Theories and Concepts

One of the main benefits of practical experience is that it allows you to apply the theories and concepts learned in the classroom to real-world situations. This can help you gain a deeper understanding of how businesses operate and how to apply your knowledge to solve real-world problems. By working on real-world projects, you can see first-hand how different business models and management theories play out in practice.

1.2.2 Development of Essential Skills

In addition to gaining a deeper understanding of the industry and business operations, practical experience can also help you develop essential skills such as critical thinking, problem-solving, and communication. These skills are crucial for success in the consulting industry, where clients look to consultants to solve complex problems and improve their operations. By working on real-world projects, you can develop your ability to think critically, identify problems, and communicate effectively with clients.

1.2.3 Industry and Client Knowledge

Practical experience can also help you develop a deeper understanding of the industry and the specific challenges facing businesses. By working on real-world projects, you can gain a better understanding of the industry and its unique characteristics and challenges. You can also gain insight into the challenges faced by specific clients and industries, which can help you provide more effective consulting services.

1.2.4 Building a Professional Network

Consulting is a relationship-based business, and building relationships with clients, colleagues, and industry leaders is essential for success. Practical experience provides you with the opportunity to build your professional network by working with a variety of clients and colleagues. By building relationships with these individuals, you can open up new opportunities for career advancement and professional growth.

1.2.5 Challenges and Opportunities for Growth

Of course, practical experience is not without its challenges. Consulting projects can be complex and demanding, and they often require you to work under tight deadlines and deal with difficult clients. However, these challenges can also be opportunities for growth and development. By overcoming these challenges, you can build your resilience and develop the skills needed to succeed in a fast-paced and dynamic industry.

In conclusion, the importance of practical experience cannot be overstated when it comes to building a successful career in business consulting. By gaining hands-on experience working on real-world projects, you can develop essential skills, build your professional network, and gain a deeper understanding of the industry and the challenges facing businesses. While practical experience can be challenging at times, the benefits far outweigh the costs.

1.3 Building Your Personal Brand

The concept of personal branding has become increasingly important in the business world, and it is a critical aspect of becoming a successful consultant. Personal branding involves creating a unique and consistent image of yourself that communicates your skills, values, and personality.

First, personal branding is crucial for consultants because it helps establish credibility and trust with clients. Clients are more likely to work with consultants who have a strong personal brand, as it demonstrates that the consultant is knowledgeable and trustworthy in their field. A strong personal brand can help differentiate you from other consultants and position you as a leader in your area of expertise.

To build your personal brand, start by identifying your unique selling proposition (USP). Your USP is the combination of your skills, experiences, and personality traits that set you apart from other consultants. To identify your USP, reflect on your strengths and weaknesses, what you are passionate about, and what makes you unique. Once you have identified your USP, you can use it to craft your personal brand messaging.

It is important to create a consistent online presence. This means having a professional website, a social media presence, and an active blog. Your website should be easy to navigate and visually appealing, and should include your USP and a clear description of the services you offer. Social media can be a powerful tool for building your personal brand, but it is important to use it strategically. Choose platforms that align with your target audience and post content that is relevant and valuable to them. Finally, an active blog can help position you as an expert in your field and provide a platform to share your thoughts and insights with your audience.

Another key aspect of personal branding is developing a strong network. Networking can help you expand your client base, find new opportunities, and establish yourself as a thought leader in your industry. Attend industry events, join professional organizations, and connect with other consultants and potential clients on social media. Building relationships with others in your field can also help you stay up to date on industry trends and best practices.

It is relevant to develop a consistent visual identity. This includes your logo, color scheme, and other design elements that represent your brand. A consistent visual identity helps establish brand recognition and makes it easier for potential clients to remember you. Consider hiring a professional designer to create a visual identity that reflects your personal brand and resonates with your target audience.

Building your personal brand is a critical aspect of becoming a successful consultant. Personal branding helps establish credibility and trust with clients, differentiate yourself from other consultants, and position yourself as a thought leader in your field. To build your personal brand, identify your USP, create a consistent online presence, develop a strong network, and establish a consistent visual identity. By following these steps, you can create a powerful personal brand that helps you stand out in a crowded consulting marketplace.

1.4 Creating a Network of Contacts

Creating a network of contacts is an essential part of building a successful career in business consulting. Having a strong network can provide a consultant with valuable resources, knowledge, and opportunities for growth. In the chapter "The Art of Business Consulting," we explore the importance of networking and provide tips on how to build and maintain a valuable network of contacts.

1.4.1 The Benefits of Networking

Networking is essential in business consulting for several reasons. First and foremost, it can help you to stay up-to-date with the latest trends and insights in your field. By connecting with other consultants, you can learn from their experiences, stay informed about industry developments, and gain new perspectives on the challenges you face.

Networking can also help you to build your reputation as a consultant. By connecting with other professionals, you can share your expertise, showcase your skills, and build a strong reputation as a trusted advisor. This can lead to new opportunities, referrals, and collaborations that can help to grow your business.

Additionally, networking can help you to find new clients. Many consultants find that their best clients come from referrals, and building a strong network can increase the chances of receiving referrals. By building relationships with other professionals who have similar or complementary expertise, you can expand your reach and increase your chances of finding new clients.

Building a strong network of contacts takes time and effort, but it is well worth the investment. Here are some tips for building and maintaining a valuable network of contacts:

- Attend networking events: Attending industry events, conferences, and trade shows can be an excellent way to connect with other professionals in your field. Make sure to come prepared with business cards and a clear elevator pitch that highlights your expertise and services.
- Join professional organizations: Joining professional organizations can be a great way to meet other professionals in your field and stay informed about industry developments. Consider joining organizations that are relevant to your

area of expertise, such as the Institute of Management Consultants or the Association of Business Process Management Professionals.

- Participate in online communities: Online communities such as LinkedIn groups and forums can be a great way to connect with other professionals and share your expertise. Make sure to engage in conversations, share valuable insights, and build relationships with other members.
- Leverage social media: Social media platforms like LinkedIn, Twitter, and Instagram can be powerful tools for building your network. Make sure to maintain a professional online presence, share valuable content, and engage with other professionals in your field.
- Offer value to others: Building relationships with other professionals is a two-way street. Make sure to offer value to others by sharing your expertise, making introductions, and providing support when needed.

Building a strong network is only half the battle. It's also important to maintain your network over time. Here are some tips for keeping in touch with your contacts and nurturing your relationships:

- Follow up regularly: Make sure to follow up with new contacts within a few days of meeting them. Send a personalized email or message thanking them for their time and expressing your interest in staying in touch.
- Schedule regular check-ins: Set reminders to check in with your contacts on a regular basis. This can be as simple as sending a quick message or email to see how they're doing and offer support if needed.
- Share valuable content: Share valuable content with your network on a regular basis. This can include articles, reports, or insights on industry developments. Make sure to personalize your messages and highlight how the content is relevant to your contact's interests or needs.
- Offer support: If you hear that a contact is facing a challenge or needs help with a project, offer your support. This can be a great way to deepen your relationship and build trust.

1.5   The Role of Certifications in Consulting

The field of business consulting is a highly competitive industry, and clients are looking for consultants who possess a high level of knowledge and expertise. One way for consultants to demonstrate their skills and abilities is through certifications. Certifications are designed to provide consultants with a clear and objective measure of their skills and knowledge in a particular area of business. In this chapter, we will discuss the role of certifications in consulting, their importance, and how they can benefit consultants and their clients.

Academic certification is important for consultants because it help to establish their credibility and expertise. Certifications are generally awarded by recognized industry bodies, and they indicate that the consultant has met a specific set of criteria, such as passing an exam or completing a certain amount of training. By obtaining certifications, consultants can demonstrate to their clients that they have the necessary skills and knowledge to provide high-quality consulting services.

Certifications can help consultants to differentiate themselves from their competitors. In a crowded consulting market, certifications can help to set a consultant apart from other consultants who may not have the same level of qualifications. This can be especially important for consultants who are just starting out in their careers and are looking to build their reputations.

It can be beneficial for clients who are looking to hire a consultant. Clients often have a limited understanding of the consulting industry and may not know how to evaluate the skills and expertise of potential consultants. Certifications provide clients with a clear and objective measure of a consultant's abilities, which can help them to make more informed decisions when selecting a consultant to work with.

There are many different types of certifications available to consultants, and the specific certifications that are relevant to a consultant will depend on their area of expertise. For example, a consultant who specializes in project management may obtain certifications such as the Project Management Professional (PMP) certification, while a consultant who specializes in finance may obtain certifications such as the Chartered Financial Analyst (CFA) certification.

Certifications are not a requirement to work as a consultant, and some consultants may choose not to obtain certifications. However, there are several benefits to obtaining certifications that make them a worthwhile investment for many consultants. One of the main benefits of certifications is that they can help to increase a consultant's earning potential. According to a survey conducted by the Institute of Management Consultants USA, consultants who hold certifications earn an average of 20% more than consultants who do not hold certifications.

In addition to increasing earning potential, certifications can also help consultants to expand their professional networks. Many industry bodies that offer certifications also provide opportunities for consultants to connect with other professionals in their field. This can be a valuable way for consultants to learn from others and to stay up-to-date on the latest industry trends and best practices.

It is important to note that obtaining certifications is not a one-time process. Many certifications require ongoing professional development and education in order to maintain the certification. This can include attending conferences, completing continuing education courses, and staying up-to-date on changes to industry regulations and standards. Consultants who hold certifications must be committed to ongoing learning and development in order to maintain their certifications and to continue to provide high-quality consulting services to their clients.

Certifications can play an important role in the field of business consulting. They provide consultants with a clear and objective measure of their skills and knowledge, help consultants to differentiate themselves from their competitors, and provide clients with the assurance that they are working with a qualified and experienced consultant. While certifications are not a requirement to work as a consultant, they can provide many benefits that make them a worthwhile investment for many consultants. If you are considering a career in consulting, it is worth exploring the certifications that are relevant to your area of expertise and considering how they can help you to achieve your professional goals.

Chapter 2
Understanding the Client

Understanding the client is a crucial aspect of business consulting. As a consultant, it is your responsibility to help clients achieve their goals and overcome their challenges. However, to do this effectively, you need to have a thorough understanding of the client's business, industry, and needs. This chapter will explore the importance of understanding the client and offer some tips and strategies for doing so.

Understanding the Client's Business Before you can offer any advice or guidance, you need to have a deep understanding of the client's business. This includes their products and services, their target market, their strengths and weaknesses, and their overall goals and objectives. Without this knowledge, you will be unable to provide meaningful insights or recommendations.

To gain a better understanding of the client's business, it can be helpful to conduct a thorough analysis of their operations. This may involve reviewing financial statements, marketing materials, and other relevant documentation. Additionally, you may need to interview key personnel within the organization to get a better sense of their culture, values, and priorities.

Understanding the Client's Industry In addition to understanding the client's business, it is important to have a thorough understanding of the industry in which they operate. This includes knowledge of industry trends, regulations, and competitive landscape. By understanding the broader context in which the client operates, you can provide more informed advice and guidance.

To gain a better understanding of the client's industry, you may need to conduct research and analysis. This may involve reviewing industry reports, attending industry conferences, or networking with other industry professionals. By staying up-to-date on the latest trends and developments, you can provide clients with valuable insights and perspectives.

© The Author(s), under exclusive license to Springer Nature Switzerland AG 2023
F. Addimando, *Client-Centered Business Consulting*, SpringerBriefs in
Psychology, https://doi.org/10.1007/978-3-031-42844-9_2

Understanding the Client's Needs Once you have a thorough understanding of the client's business and industry, it is important to identify their specific needs and challenges. This requires careful listening and empathy, as well as the ability to ask the right questions.

To understand the client's needs, it can be helpful to conduct a needs assessment or discovery process. This may involve surveys, interviews, or other data collection methods. By gathering information directly from the client, you can ensure that your recommendations are tailored to their specific needs and priorities.

Tips for Understanding the Client To effectively understand the client, there are several tips and strategies that can be helpful. These include:

- Active listening: Paying attention to what the client is saying and asking follow-up questions to clarify their needs.
- Empathy: Putting yourself in the client's shoes and understanding their perspective.
- Curiosity: Being curious about the client's business and asking questions to learn more.
- Objectivity: Maintaining a neutral and objective perspective, even when discussing sensitive or emotional topics.
- Flexibility: Being willing to adjust your approach based on the client's needs and preferences.

By following these tips and strategies, you can develop a strong understanding of the client and provide them with valuable advice and guidance. These include:

- More effective solutions: By tailoring your recommendations to the client's specific needs and challenges, you can offer more effective solutions.
- Increased trust: By demonstrating that you understand the client's business and industry, you can build trust and credibility.
- Better communication: By understanding the client's perspective and needs, you can communicate more effectively and avoid misunderstandings.
- Improved outcomes: By providing more effective solutions, you can help the client achieve their goals and improve their overall outcomes.

In conclusion, understanding the client is a critical aspect of business consulting. By developing a deep understanding of the client's business, industry, and needs, you can provide more effective solutions and improve outcomes.

2.1 The Psychology of Decision-Making

The psychology of decision-making is a crucial topic in the field of business consulting. As consultants, it is important to understand how clients make decisions in order to provide effective advice and recommendations. Decision-making is a complex process that is influenced by a variety of factors, including cognitive biases, emotions, and social pressures. By understanding these factors, consultants can help clients make more informed and rational decisions that are in line with their goals.

One of the key aspects of the psychology of decision-making is cognitive biases. These are unconscious mental shortcuts that our brains use to make decisions more quickly and efficiently. However, these shortcuts can also lead to errors in judgement and decision-making. For example, confirmation bias is the tendency to seek out information that confirms our existing beliefs and discount information that contradicts them. Consultants must be aware of these biases and help clients to overcome them by gathering and considering all relevant information.

Another important factor in decision-making is emotion. Emotions can influence decisions in a variety of ways, from driving impulsive actions to clouding judgement. For example, a client may be hesitant to make a difficult decision because of fear or anxiety. Consultants must be able to recognize these emotional influences and help clients to manage them in order to make rational decisions.

Social pressures can also play a role in decision-making. Clients may feel pressure from peers, superiors, or other stakeholders to make decisions that are not in their best interests. Consultants must be aware of these pressures and help clients to consider their own goals and priorities in the decision-making process.

In addition to understanding the factors that influence decision-making, consultants must also be skilled in helping clients to evaluate options and make decisions. This requires strong analytical skills, as well as the ability to communicate complex information in a clear and concise manner. Consultants must also be able to work collaboratively with clients to develop solutions that meet their needs and align with their goals.

One approach that consultants can use to help clients make decisions is decision analysis. This is a structured approach that involves breaking down complex decisions into smaller, more manageable pieces. Consultants can use decision analysis to help clients identify all relevant factors, evaluate options, and weigh the pros and cons of each option. This approach can help clients to make more informed and rational decisions that are based on a thorough understanding of the situation.

Another important aspect of the psychology of decision-making is the concept of risk. Clients may be hesitant to take risks or may be overly risk-seeking, depending on their individual personalities and attitudes. Consultants must be able to help clients to understand the risks associated with different options and develop strategies for managing those risks. This may involve conducting risk assessments, developing contingency plans, or exploring alternative options that may be less risky.

Finally, it is important for consultants to understand the role of intuition in decision-making. While decision-making should always be based on a thorough analysis of all relevant factors, intuition can also play a role in guiding decisions. Intuition is based on years of experience and can provide valuable insights that may not be immediately apparent from an analysis of the data. However, it is important to balance intuition with analysis to ensure that decisions are based on a solid foundation of evidence and information.

The psychology of decision-making is a critical topic for business consultants. By understanding the factors that influence decision-making, consultants can help clients to make more informed and rational decisions that are aligned with their goals. This requires a combination of analytical skills, communication skills, and an understanding of human psychology. By mastering these skills, consultants can provide valuable advice and guidance to clients that can help them to achieve their business objectives.

2.2 Understanding the Client's Needs

Understanding the client's needs is a crucial component of successful business consulting. In order to provide effective and valuable advice, consultants must have a clear understanding of what their clients require. This involves identifying the client's goals, challenges, pain points, and priorities, as well as understanding their industry, competition, and market dynamics.

To gain a deeper understanding of the client's needs, consultants should begin by conducting a thorough needs assessment. This process involves a series of meetings, interviews, and data analysis to identify the key issues and challenges facing the client's organization. The needs assessment typically involves the following steps:

- Define the problem: The consultant must clearly define the problem that the client is facing. This involves identifying the symptoms, root causes, and implications of the problem. Defining the problem is a critical step as it sets the stage for the rest of the engagement.
- Gather information: The consultant must gather information about the client's organization, including its structure, culture, processes, and systems. This information can be obtained through interviews with key stakeholders, document reviews, and data analysis.
- Analyze the data: The consultant must analyze the data collected to identify the root causes of the problem. This involves identifying patterns, trends, and anomalies that may be contributing to the problem.
- Develop recommendations: Based on the analysis, the consultant must develop a set of recommendations that address the root causes of the problem. These recommendations should be practical, actionable, and tailored to the client's specific needs.

Once the needs assessment is complete, the consultant can work with the client to develop a customized consulting engagement that meets their needs. This engagement may involve a range of activities, such as strategy development, process improvement, organizational design, or technology implementation.

To effectively understand the client's needs, consultants must also be skilled in active listening and effective communication. This involves asking the right questions, listening carefully to the client's responses, and clarifying any misunderstandings. Active listening and effective communication help build trust and credibility with the client, which is essential for a successful consulting engagement.

Another key aspect of understanding the client's needs is being able to anticipate their future needs. This involves staying up-to-date on industry trends, emerging technologies, and changing customer preferences. By anticipating the client's future needs, consultants can help the client stay ahead of the competition and achieve long-term success.

It is also important for consultants to understand the client's business model, revenue streams, and financial metrics. This understanding helps the consultant develop recommendations that are aligned with the client's financial goals and constraints.

In addition to understanding the client's needs, consultants must also be able to manage their expectations. Clients often have high expectations for the outcome of the consulting engagement, and it is the consultant's responsibility to ensure that these expectations are realistic and achievable. This involves setting clear objectives and timelines, communicating progress regularly, and managing any potential scope creep.

Understanding the client's needs is a critical component of successful business consulting. Consultants must be skilled in conducting a thorough needs assessment, active listening, effective communication, and anticipating future needs. By understanding the client's needs, consultants can develop customized solutions that meet their specific goals and challenges and help them achieve long-term success.

2.3   Building Rapport and Trust

Building rapport and trust are two critical components of successful business consulting. Rapport refers to the relationship, understanding, and connection between the consultant and the client. Trust, on the other hand, refers to the confidence and reliability that the client has in the consultant's skills, knowledge, and intentions.

Building rapport and trust requires a consultant to establish and maintain a positive and respectful relationship with the client. It involves being an active listener, understanding the client's needs and concerns, and communicating effectively to ensure that the client feels heard and understood. It also involves demonstrating professionalism, competence, and integrity in all interactions with the client.

One key way to build rapport and trust is to establish clear and open communication from the outset. This involves setting expectations and goals for the consulting relationship, as well as establishing a clear line of communication that allows the client to contact the consultant as needed. It also involves being responsive and proactive in addressing the client's questions, concerns, and feedback.

Another important factor in building rapport and trust is to demonstrate empathy and emotional intelligence. This means understanding the client's perspective and emotions, and being able to relate to them in a genuine and authentic way. It also means being able to adapt to the client's communication style and preferences and tailor the consulting approach to meet their needs.

Trust is also built through the consultant's competence and expertise. This involves demonstrating a thorough understanding of the client's industry and business needs, as well as having the technical skills and knowledge necessary to provide effective solutions and recommendations. It also involves being transparent and honest in all interactions with the client and being willing to admit when there are areas of uncertainty or when mistakes are made.

Another important aspect of building trust is establishing credibility and a strong reputation in the consulting industry. This involves cultivating positive relationships with other consultants, industry experts, and thought leaders, as well as staying up-to-date on industry trends and best practices. It also means having a track record of successful consulting engagements and being able to provide references and testimonials from satisfied clients.

In order to build and maintain rapport and trust, it is also important for the consultant to be reliable and consistent in their approach. This means following through on commitments and deadlines, being punctual and prepared for meetings, and demonstrating a commitment to ongoing communication and feedback.

Finally, building rapport and trust requires a long-term approach to the consulting relationship. This means investing time and effort in understanding the client's business, industry, and culture and building a relationship based on mutual respect, understanding, and trust. It also means being willing to adapt and evolve the consulting approach over time, as the client's needs and priorities change.

Building rapport and trust are critical components of successful business consulting. It requires a consultant to establish and maintain a positive and respectful relationship with the client, communicate effectively, demonstrate empathy and emotional intelligence, and establish credibility and a strong reputation in the consulting industry. It also requires a long-term approach to the consulting relationship, with a focus on ongoing communication, feedback, and adaptation to the client's evolving needs and priorities.

2.4   Dealing with Difficult Clients

As a business consultant, it is important to know how to deal with difficult clients. Difficult clients can be a major source of stress, frustration, and conflict, which can make it difficult to deliver effective consulting services. However, with the right approach, it is possible to handle difficult clients in a way that maintains positive relationships and helps to achieve the goals of the consulting engagement.

The first step in dealing with difficult clients is to understand why they are being difficult. There are a number of reasons why clients may be difficult to work with, including personality conflicts, unrealistic expectations, communication breakdowns, and resistance to change. By understanding the root causes of the difficulty, consultants can begin to develop strategies for managing the situation.

One effective approach for dealing with difficult clients is to establish clear expectations from the outset of the consulting engagement. This can help to prevent misunderstandings and ensure that both parties are on the same page. Consultants should be clear about the scope of their services, the timeline for the engagement, and the expected outcomes. They should also be clear about their own responsibilities and what they need from the client in order to be successful.

Communication is key when it comes to dealing with difficult clients. It is important to establish regular communication channels and to keep the client informed of progress and any issues that arise. This can help to prevent misunderstandings and ensure that the client feels involved in the process. Consultants should also be open to feedback and willing to listen to the client's concerns.

Another effective strategy for dealing with difficult clients is to be proactive in addressing issues as they arise. This can help to prevent minor issues from escalating into major conflicts. Consultants should be willing to acknowledge mistakes and take responsibility for any issues that arise. They should also be proactive in addressing any concerns or complaints that the client may have.

It is also important to remain calm and professional when dealing with difficult clients. It can be easy to become frustrated or defensive when dealing with a difficult client, but this will only exacerbate the situation. Instead, consultants should remain calm and focused on finding a solution to the problem. They should also avoid taking the client's behavior personally and should remain respectful and professional at all times.

It is important to know when to walk away from a difficult client. While it is important to try to work through difficulties and maintain positive relationships, there may be situations where it is simply not possible to achieve the goals of the engagement. In these cases, it may be necessary to terminate the engagement or to refer the client to another consultant who may be better suited to their needs.

In conclusion, dealing with difficult clients is an important part of business consulting. By understanding the root causes of difficulty, establishing clear expectations, maintaining regular communication, being proactive in addressing issues, remaining calm and professional, and knowing when to walk away, consultants can effectively manage difficult clients and maintain positive relationships. The ability to handle difficult clients is an important skill for any business consultant, and with practice and experience, it is a skill that can be developed and honed over time.

2.5 Maintaining Client Relationships

Maintaining client relationships is an essential aspect of business consulting. In this section, we will discuss the importance of building a long-term relationship with clients, effective communication strategies, and maintaining trust and credibility.

Building long-term relationships with clients is critical in business consulting. It involves not only meeting their immediate needs but also providing value-added services that ensure continued success. By building a long-term relationship, consultants can create a loyal client base that will continue to work with them over time.

This, in turn, will help consultants to build their reputation, increase referrals, and secure future business.

Effective communication is the foundation of maintaining client relationships. It is important to communicate regularly, clearly, and effectively with clients to build trust and credibility. Regular communication can help to ensure that clients are kept informed about the progress of the project, any changes or issues, and any potential risks or opportunities that may arise. It also allows consultants to identify any problems or concerns early and address them promptly, thereby reducing the likelihood of escalation.

It is important to understand that effective communication involves not just talking but also listening. Listening is an essential aspect of communication and helps consultants to understand the client's perspective, needs, and concerns. This, in turn, helps to build trust and credibility as clients feel that they are being heard and understood. Active listening involves paying attention to not just what the client is saying but also their nonverbal cues and body language.

Building trust and credibility is an important part of maintaining client relationships. Trust is built over time by consistently delivering on promises and meeting or exceeding client expectations. It is important to be honest, transparent, and ethical in all business dealings. Consultants must also ensure that they are responsive to clients' needs and concerns and take prompt action to address any issues or problems.

Another way to build trust is by delivering value-added services that go beyond what was initially agreed upon. This may include providing additional insights or recommendations that can help to improve the client's business operations or solve a problem that they are facing. It is important to demonstrate that consultants are invested in the client's success and are willing to go the extra mile to help them achieve their goals.

In addition to building trust and credibility, maintaining client relationships also involves managing expectations. Consultants must be clear about what they can and cannot deliver and ensure that clients have realistic expectations about what can be achieved. Managing expectations involves setting clear goals and objectives and being transparent about the limitations of the project or engagement.

Managing expectations also involves being honest about potential risks and challenges that may arise during the project. It is important to be proactive in identifying and addressing any potential issues or risks that may arise and to keep clients informed throughout the process. This helps to build trust and credibility as clients feel that they are being kept in the loop and are aware of any potential risks or challenges.

Another aspect of maintaining client relationships is managing conflicts. Conflict is a natural part of any business relationship and can arise due to differences in expectations, goals, or communication styles. It is important to address conflicts proactively and find a resolution that is satisfactory to both parties. This may involve finding a compromise or solution that meets both parties' needs, or it may involve terminating the relationship if the conflict cannot be resolved.

Maintaining client relationships is a critical aspect of business consulting. Effective communication, building trust and credibility, managing expectations, and managing conflicts are all important elements of maintaining long-term relationships with clients. Consultants must be proactive in addressing clients' needs and concerns, delivering value-added services, and building a loyal client base that will continue to work with them over time. By doing so, they can build their reputation, increase referrals, and secure future business.

2.6   Understanding Human Psychology in Business Consulting

2.6.1   Introduction to Human Psychology in Consulting

In the realm of business consulting, the ability to understand and navigate human psychology is a vital skill for consultants seeking to build successful client relationships and deliver effective solutions. Human psychology encompasses the study of how individuals think, feel, and behave, providing invaluable insights into the motivations, needs, and decision-making processes of clients.

By delving into this subject, consultants can develop a deeper understanding of their clients, enhance their rapport-building skills, and tailor their consulting approach to meet clients' specific needs. At its core, human psychology in consulting revolves around the concept of empathy. Empathy is the capacity to understand and share the emotions, perspectives, and experiences of others. For consultants, empathy is a critical tool for establishing trust and connection with clients. By demonstrating empathy, consultants can create an environment where clients feel understood, valued, and supported.

One aspect of human psychology that consultants must consider is emotional intelligence (EI). Emotional intelligence refers to the ability to recognize, understand, and manage one's own emotions, as well as to perceive and empathize with the emotions of others. Consultants with high emotional intelligence possess the skills necessary to navigate the complexities of client interactions and adapt their approach accordingly. They are adept at recognizing and regulating their own emotions, allowing them to stay composed, focused, and attentive during client engagements.

Furthermore, emotional intelligence enables consultants to empathize with clients, understanding their concerns, fears, and aspirations. This empathetic understanding facilitates effective communication, builds trust, and establishes a strong foundation for collaborative problem-solving. Daniel Goleman's framework of emotional intelligence highlights key components that consultants can develop to enhance their emotional intelligence.

Self-awareness is the foundation of emotional intelligence, involving an understanding of one's own emotions, strengths, weaknesses, and triggers. By cultivating self-awareness, consultants can identify their emotional states and how these may influence their interactions with clients. Self-regulation is the ability to manage and control one's emotions and responses effectively. Consultants with strong self-regulation skills can remain calm and composed in challenging situations, ensuring that their emotions do not hinder the consulting process.

Motivation is another component of emotional intelligence, driving consultants to deliver high-quality results and maintain a positive attitude even in the face of obstacles. Consultants who possess a genuine passion for their work and a desire to make a difference are more likely to inspire and engage their clients.

Empathy is a crucial aspect of emotional intelligence that allows consultants to understand and resonate with clients' emotions and perspectives. By developing empathy, consultants can create a safe and supportive space where clients feel comfortable expressing their concerns, goals, and aspirations.

Active listening is a valuable tool in cultivating empathy, as it involves fully engaging with clients, demonstrating genuine interest, and seeking to understand their needs, desires, and challenges. Consultants who actively listen are better equipped to identify underlying issues, uncover hidden motivations, and provide tailored recommendations that address clients' unique circumstances.

Another psychological framework that consultants can employ is Abraham Maslow's Hierarchy of Needs. Maslow's theory posits that individuals have a series of needs that must be fulfilled in a specific order. At the base of the hierarchy are physiological needs, such as food, water, and shelter. As these needs are met, individuals progress to seeking safety, belongingness, esteem, and, ultimately, self-actualization.

Understanding where clients are positioned within Maslow's Hierarchy of Needs can help consultants tailor their approach and recommendations accordingly. For example, if a client is primarily concerned with financial stability and security, consultants can focus on providing solutions that address these needs before delving into higher-level aspirations such as personal growth or self-actualization.

By aligning their consulting efforts with clients' fundamental needs, consultants can establish a strong rapport, demonstrate their understanding, and create strategies that resonate with clients' aspirations.

Understanding human psychology in consulting also involves recognizing the influence of cognitive biases on clients' decision-making processes. Cognitive biases are systematic patterns of deviation from rationality or objectivity in judgment, often leading individuals to make decisions based on subjective factors rather than objective analysis. As a consultant, being aware of these biases can help you understand how clients perceive information, make choices, and respond to your recommendations. One common cognitive bias is confirmation bias, which refers to the tendency to seek and interpret information in a way that confirms existing beliefs or preconceived notions.

Clients may selectively focus on information that aligns with their preferences or biases, potentially hindering their ability to consider alternative perspectives or solutions. As a consultant, it is crucial to present a balanced view of the situation, provide diverse insights, and encourage clients to critically evaluate different options.

Anchoring bias is another cognitive bias that can significantly impact decision-making. It involves relying heavily on the initial information or reference point presented when making judgments or choices. Consultants should be mindful of this bias and carefully consider the information they present at the onset of a consulting engagement. By providing well-reasoned and objective information from the outset, consultants can help clients avoid anchoring their decisions solely on the initial information.

The availability heuristic is yet another cognitive bias that affects decision-making. It refers to the tendency to overestimate the importance of information that is easily accessible or readily available. Clients may heavily rely on information that comes to mind easily, rather than considering a broader range of data or perspectives.

As a consultant, it is important to encourage clients to explore and analyze a wide array of relevant information, ensuring that decisions are based on a comprehensive understanding of the situation. In addition to cognitive biases, consultants can also draw insights from the field of behavioral economics, which combines elements of psychology and economics to understand how individuals make economic decisions. Behavioral economics provides valuable insights into the ways in which individuals' choices are influenced by factors such as social norms, framing effects, and loss aversion.

One concept within behavioral economics that can be particularly relevant to consulting is nudging. Nudging involves subtly influencing people's behavior by structuring choices and presenting information in a way that guides them toward desired outcomes. Consultants can apply the principles of nudging to help clients adopt beneficial behaviors or make optimal decisions.

For instance, by framing choices in a way that emphasizes long-term benefits or by using social proof to demonstrate how others have achieved success, consultants can positively influence clients' decision-making processes and encourage the adoption of effective strategies. Effective communication is a cornerstone of understanding human psychology in consulting. Consultants should be skilled communicators, able to convey complex ideas and recommendations in a clear and concise manner. The use of language, both verbal and nonverbal, plays a crucial role in communication.

Consultants should be mindful of their tone, body language, and facial expressions, as these can impact how clients perceive and interpret their messages. By adapting their communication style to the preferences of their clients, consultants can foster stronger connections and ensure that their recommendations are effectively understood and implemented. Active listening is another essential aspect of effective communication. It involves not only hearing what clients are saying but also actively engaging with their ideas, concerns, and aspirations.

By demonstrating active listening through paraphrasing, clarifying, and reflecting on clients' statements, consultants can show their clients that they are genuinely interested in understanding their needs and perspectives. Active listening fosters trust, encourages open dialogue, and enables consultants to gain valuable insights that can inform their recommendations.

An understanding of human psychology is crucial for consultants seeking to build successful client relationships and deliver effective solutions. By incorporating principles from emotional intelligence, Maslow's Hierarchy of Needs, cognitive biases, and behavioral economics, consultants can develop a deeper understanding of their clients' motivations, needs, and decision-making processes.

This understanding allows consultants to tailor their approach, effectively communicate, and provide valuable insights and recommendations that resonate with clients. By cultivating empathy and emotional intelligence, consultants can establish a strong rapport with clients, creating an environment of trust and understanding.

They can actively listen to clients' concerns, aspirations, and challenges, enabling them to provide tailored solutions that address clients' unique circumstances. Additionally, consultants can draw upon Abraham Maslow's Hierarchy of Needs to understand where clients are positioned in their journey and tailor their recommendations accordingly. By addressing clients' fundamental needs first, consultants can establish a solid foundation and then guide clients toward higher-level aspirations and goals. Being aware of cognitive biases that influence decision-making is critical for consultants.

By recognizing biases such as confirmation bias, anchoring bias, and availability heuristic, consultants can present balanced information, encourage critical thinking, and help clients make more informed decisions. Insights from behavioral economics can also inform consultants' strategies. By understanding how social norms, framing effects, and loss aversion impact decision-making, consultants can structure choices and present information in a way that nudges clients toward desired outcomes. Effective communication, both verbal and nonverbal, is essential for consultants to convey their ideas and recommendations clearly.

Adapting communication styles to clients' preferences and actively listening to their needs and perspectives fosters stronger connections and ensures effective information transfer. In conclusion, an introduction to human psychology in consulting provides consultants with invaluable insights into their clients' motivations, needs, and decision-making processes.

By incorporating principles from empathy, emotional intelligence, Maslow's Hierarchy of Needs, cognitive biases, and behavioral economics, consultants can enhance their understanding and ability to deliver tailored solutions that resonate with clients. By cultivating strong client relationships based on trust, effective communication, and an understanding of clients' unique circumstances, consultants can drive meaningful and impactful outcomes for their clients' businesses.

2.7   The Role of Emotional Intelligence

Emotional intelligence (EI) plays a significant role in various aspects of life, and its importance is particularly pronounced in the realm of business and professional relationships. In the context of consulting, emotional intelligence is a vital skill that can greatly influence a consultant's effectiveness in building rapport, understanding client needs, and delivering successful outcomes.

By comprehending the role of emotional intelligence and actively developing this skill set, consultants can enhance their interactions, cultivate stronger relationships, and ultimately achieve greater success in their consulting engagements.

At its core, emotional intelligence refers to the ability to recognize, understand, and manage one's own emotions, as well as to perceive and empathize with the emotions of others. It encompasses a range of competencies, including self-awareness, self-regulation, motivation, empathy, and social skills.

These components work together to shape an individual's emotional intelligence and greatly impact their interactions with clients. Self-awareness is the foundation of emotional intelligence. It involves having a clear understanding of one's own emotions, strengths, weaknesses, values, and triggers. Self-aware consultants are in tune with their own emotions and can effectively regulate them during client engagements.

They understand how their emotions may influence their perceptions, judgments, and decision-making processes, allowing them to maintain composure, objectivity, and professionalism even in challenging situations. Self-awareness also enables consultants to recognize their own limitations and seek support or resources when needed. Self-regulation is the ability to manage and control one's own emotions and responses effectively. Consultants with strong self-regulation skills can remain calm, composed, and level-headed, regardless of the circumstances.

They can adapt to changing client dynamics and handle unexpected challenges with grace. Self-regulation also involves being mindful of one's own behavior and communication style, ensuring that interactions with clients are respectful, professional, and focused on the client's needs. Motivation is another crucial component of emotional intelligence. Motivated consultants possess a genuine passion for their work and a deep sense of purpose.

They are driven to deliver high-quality results, continuously improve their skills, and make a meaningful impact on their clients' businesses. Motivation not only fuels consultants' own personal and professional growth but also inspires and energizes their clients.

A motivated consultant can instill confidence and optimism in clients, driving them to actively engage in the consulting process and embrace positive changes. Empathy is a fundamental aspect of emotional intelligence that has profound implications for consulting. Empathy is the ability to understand and share the emotions, perspectives, and experiences of others. For consultants, empathy is a powerful tool for building rapport, establishing trust, and creating an environment where clients feel understood, valued, and supported.

By empathizing with clients, consultants can develop a deep understanding of their needs, concerns, and aspirations. This understanding allows consultants to tailor their recommendations, communication style, and approach to address clients' specific circumstances, thereby increasing the likelihood of successful outcomes.

Effective empathy involves active listening, observing nonverbal cues, and demonstrating genuine care and understanding. It requires consultants to put themselves in their clients' shoes, considering their challenges, motivations, and goals. By adopting an empathetic stance, consultants can create a safe and supportive space for clients to share their thoughts, emotions, and uncertainties.

This empathetic connection fosters trust, encourages open communication, and enables consultants to collaboratively develop solutions that truly meet clients' needs. Social skills are the final component of emotional intelligence and encompass a range of interpersonal abilities. Consultants with strong social skills excel in building and maintaining relationships, navigating social dynamics, and effectively communicating with diverse stakeholders. Socially skilled consultants are adept at networking, collaborating, and influencing others.

They can effectively manage client expectations, resolve conflicts, and facilitate productive discussions. These skills enable consultants to work seamlessly with clients, stakeholders, and team members, creating a harmonious and collaborative environment that fosters collective success. In the context of consulting, social skills are crucial for establishing rapport with clients and creating a positive client experience. Consultants with strong social skills are able to establish a sense of trust and credibility with their clients from the very beginning. They are skilled at engaging in active and attentive listening, allowing clients to feel heard and understood.

By fostering open and transparent communication, consultants can build strong relationships based on mutual respect and collaboration. Furthermore, social skills play a vital role in effectively managing client expectations. Consultants must be able to clearly communicate project timelines, deliverables, and any potential challenges that may arise. By setting realistic expectations and maintaining open lines of communication, consultants can prevent misunderstandings, build trust, and ensure client satisfaction throughout the engagement.

Consultants with well-developed emotional intelligence also excel in team environments. They possess the ability to understand and navigate group dynamics, facilitate effective communication, and build cohesive and high-performing teams. Emotional intelligence allows consultants to recognize and leverage the unique strengths and perspectives of each team member, promoting a collaborative and inclusive work environment.

By fostering a sense of psychological safety and promoting open dialogue, emotionally intelligent consultants can create an atmosphere where team members feel comfortable expressing their ideas and concerns, leading to more innovative solutions and improved project outcomes.

Moreover, emotional intelligence can be particularly valuable when dealing with challenging or difficult clients. In consulting, consultants may encounter clients who are resistant to change, skeptical of the consulting process, or overwhelmed by the complexities of their business challenges. By applying emotional intelligence, consultants can navigate these challenging situations with empathy, patience, and understanding. They can adapt their approach to meet the client's emotional needs, address their concerns, and guide them toward embracing positive change. By demonstrating emotional intelligence, consultants can turn potentially difficult clients into collaborative partners, enhancing the overall success of the engagement.

Developing emotional intelligence is a lifelong journey that requires self-reflection, practice, and continuous growth. There are several strategies that consultants can employ to enhance their emotional intelligence:

- Self-reflection: Regularly taking the time to reflect on one's own emotions, reactions, and behaviors can deepen self-awareness and provide insights into areas for growth and development.
- Emotional regulation techniques: Learning and practicing techniques such as deep breathing, mindfulness, and meditation can help consultants effectively manage their own emotions and remain calm and composed in challenging situations.
- Active listening and empathy: Actively listening to clients, observing their non-verbal cues, and genuinely seeking to understand their perspectives fosters empathy and strengthens client relationships.
- Seeking feedback: Welcoming and seeking feedback from clients, colleagues, and supervisors can provide valuable insights into areas for improvement and help consultants enhance their emotional intelligence.
- Continuous learning: Engaging in professional development activities, such as attending workshops, reading books on emotional intelligence, or participating in coaching or mentoring programs, can support ongoing growth and development in this area.

In conclusion, emotional intelligence plays a critical role in consulting by enabling consultants to build strong client relationships, understand client needs, navigate challenging situations, and foster effective teamwork. By cultivating self-awareness, self-regulation, motivation, empathy, and social skills, consultants can enhance their effectiveness and deliver exceptional value to their clients. Developing emotional intelligence is an ongoing process that requires dedication and practice, but the rewards are significant – both in terms of personal and professional success in the consulting field.

2.8 Maslow's Hierarchy of Needs

Maslow's Hierarchy of Needs is a renowned psychological theory that provides valuable insights into the fundamental drivers of human behavior and motivation. Developed by psychologist Abraham Maslow in the mid-twentieth century, this theory proposes that individuals have a set of hierarchical needs that must be satisfied in a specific order to achieve personal growth and self-actualization.

Understanding Maslow's Hierarchy of Needs can be immensely beneficial for consultants as it helps them comprehend the underlying motivations and aspirations of their clients, tailor their approach, and design effective strategies that align with their clients' needs. The hierarchy is often depicted as a pyramid, with five distinct levels, each representing a different category of needs.

These levels, from the bottom to the top of the pyramid, are physiological needs, safety needs, belongingness and love needs, esteem needs, and self-actualization needs. At the base of the pyramid are physiological needs, which encompass the most basic requirements for human survival, such as food, water, shelter, and sleep.

These needs form the foundation upon which all other needs are built. In a consulting context, understanding the importance of physiological needs can help consultants recognize the significance of financial stability, job security, and work-life balance for their clients. Consultants can address these needs by ensuring that their recommendations and strategies do not compromise their clients' basic physiological well-being.

The next level in the hierarchy is safety needs. Safety needs refer to the need for physical and psychological security, stability, and protection from harm. In a consulting engagement, consultants must be aware of their clients' desire for stability and risk mitigation. Clients may seek guidance on issues such as crisis management, compliance with regulations, or the establishment of robust business processes.

By acknowledging and addressing safety needs, consultants can instill a sense of security and confidence in their clients, enabling them to focus on higher-level needs. The third level of Maslow's Hierarchy of Needs is belongingness and love needs. These needs encompass the desire for social connections, relationships, and a sense of belonging within a community. In a consulting context, consultants must recognize the significance of fostering positive interpersonal relationships, both within the client organization and with external stakeholders. By creating an inclusive and collaborative environment, consultants can help clients develop strong team dynamics, build effective networks, and foster a sense of belonging. Consultants can also facilitate the development of customer relationships and partnerships to meet clients' belongingness and love needs.

The fourth level comprises esteem needs, which include the desire for self-esteem, recognition, achievement, and respect from others. Esteem needs are driven by the need for self-worth and the desire for a positive self-image. In a consulting engagement, consultants can support clients in achieving their esteem needs by recognizing their achievements, providing positive feedback, and highlighting their strengths. Consultants can help clients develop strategies to enhance their reputation, establish thought leadership, and gain recognition within their industry.

By addressing esteem needs, consultants contribute to their clients' overall sense of accomplishment and self-worth. The pinnacle of Maslow's Hierarchy of Needs is self-actualization needs. Self-actualization represents the highest level of human motivation, where individuals strive to reach their full potential, pursue personal growth, and fulfill their unique talents and aspirations. Consultants can play a transformative role by guiding clients on a path of self-actualization.

This involves understanding clients' long-term visions, personal goals, and aspirations. Consultants can help clients align their business objectives with their personal values, develop strategies for growth and innovation, and support them in embracing new challenges and opportunities.

Applying Maslow's Hierarchy of Needs in consulting requires a deep understanding of clients' motivations, aspirations, and current needs. Consultants must actively listen, ask probing questions, and conduct thorough assessments to gain insight into each client's position within the hierarchy and the specific needs they seek to fulfill. Here are some key considerations and implications of Maslow's Hierarchy of Needs in the consulting context:

- Tailoring strategies: By understanding where clients fall within the hierarchy, consultants can tailor their strategies and recommendations to address the specific needs of each client. For example, if a client is primarily concerned with physiological and safety needs, consultants may need to focus on risk mitigation, cost reduction, and operational efficiency. On the other hand, clients seeking self-actualization may require guidance on innovation, leadership development, and strategic expansion.
- Value proposition: Consultants can enhance their value proposition by explicitly addressing their clients' needs at each level of the hierarchy. Clearly articulating how their services meet these needs will resonate with clients and demonstrate a deep understanding of their motivations. Consultants can highlight how their expertise and recommendations contribute to improving the overall well-being, growth, and self-actualization of their clients.
- Building trust and rapport: Understanding the underlying needs of clients helps consultants build trust and rapport. By acknowledging and addressing clients' basic physiological and safety needs, consultants create a foundation of trust and credibility. As consultants progress to addressing higher-level needs, such as belongingness and esteem, they foster stronger relationships and deeper connections with their clients, leading to increased collaboration and engagement.
- Managing resistance to change: Change can often be met with resistance, as it disrupts individuals' sense of safety and stability. By recognizing and addressing clients' safety needs, consultants can mitigate resistance to change and create a supportive environment. Communicating the potential benefits of change, providing clear guidelines and support, and ensuring open lines of communication can help clients feel secure throughout the consulting process.
- Long-term partnerships: Maslow's Hierarchy of Needs also has implications for establishing long-term partnerships with clients. By addressing their clients' needs at each level of the hierarchy, consultants can foster a sense of loyalty and ongoing engagement. As clients progress in their journey toward self-actualization, consultants can continue to provide guidance, support personal growth, and help clients navigate new challenges and opportunities.

It is important to note that Maslow's Hierarchy of Needs is not a rigid framework, and individuals may have different priorities and progress through the hierarchy at varying speeds. Moreover, individuals may have needs at multiple levels simultaneously. Consultants should approach each client with an open mind, recognizing their unique circumstances and motivations.

Maslow's Hierarchy of Needs provides a valuable framework for understanding human motivation and its implications in consulting. By recognizing and addressing clients' physiological, safety, belongingness, esteem, and self-actualization needs, consultants can effectively tailor their approach, build strong relationships, and help clients achieve their goals. Integrating this understanding of human motivation into the consulting process allows consultants to create strategies that not only drive business success but also support clients in their journey toward self-fulfillment and personal growth.

2.9   Behavioral Economics and Nudging

Behavioral economics, a field that combines principles from psychology and economics, has gained significant attention in recent years for its insights into human decision-making processes. It recognizes that individuals often deviate from rationality and are influenced by cognitive biases, emotions, and social factors when making choices. Within the context of consulting, understanding behavioral economics can be a powerful tool for consultants to help their clients make better decisions and achieve desired outcomes. One specific application of behavioral economics that has gained prominence is the concept of "nudging."

Nudging, as popularized by Nobel laureate Richard Thaler and legal scholar Cass Sunstein, refers to the use of subtle, noncoercive interventions to influence people's choices and behavior in a predictable way. Nudges aim to steer individuals toward making decisions that are in their best interest or align with specific goals, without restricting their freedom of choice. By leveraging insights from behavioral economics, consultants can design nudges that facilitate positive change and drive desired outcomes for their clients.

The key principles and techniques of behavioral economics and nudging that can be applied in the consulting context are as follows:

A. *Understanding cognitive biases:* Behavioral economics highlights the numerous cognitive biases that affect decision-making, such as loss aversion, status quo bias, and anchoring. Consultants can help clients recognize these biases and understand how they influence their decision-making processes. By doing so, consultants can provide guidance on how to overcome biases and make more informed choices.

B. *Framing and choice architecture:* How information is presented, or framed, significantly impacts decision-making. Consultants can employ framing techniques to influence clients' perceptions and preferences. By carefully structuring the choice architecture, consultants can emphasize certain aspects, highlight benefits, and reframe options to guide clients toward desirable outcomes.

C. *Defaults and opt-out provisions:* Leveraging the power of defaults is another effective nudge strategy. By setting default options that align with clients' goals, consultants can encourage clients to opt for preferred choices without imposing any restrictions. For example, consultants can recommend default settings for retirement savings plans that promote higher contribution rates, increasing the likelihood of long-term financial security.

D. *Social norms and social proof:* People are strongly influenced by social norms and tend to conform to what others are doing. Consultants can utilize social proof by highlighting positive behaviors and practices within a client's industry or peer group. By demonstrating that others have successfully adopted certain strategies or solutions, consultants can nudge clients toward making similar choices.

E. *Feedback and personalized information:* Behavioral economics emphasizes the importance of timely feedback and personalized information in influencing behavior. Consultants can implement feedback mechanisms that provide clients with real-time information about their progress, performance, or outcomes. This can help clients track their behavior, stay motivated, and make adjustments as needed.

F. *Incentives and rewards:* Consultants can design incentive structures that encourage desired behaviors and discourage undesirable ones. By aligning incentives with clients' goals and values, consultants can nudge clients toward actions that lead to positive outcomes. Incentives can be monetary or nonmonetary, such as recognition, privileges, or social benefits.

G. *Choice simplification and defaults:* Decision-making can be overwhelming when faced with numerous options. Consultants can simplify choices by reducing complexity and providing clear, concise information. Consultants can also help clients identify and prioritize their goals, enabling them to focus on the most important decisions.

H. *Nudges for sustainable behavior:* Behavioral economics can be applied to encourage sustainable practices within organizations. By implementing nudges that promote energy conservation, waste reduction, or environmentally friendly behaviors, consultants can help clients align their operations with sustainable objectives.

Consultants should approach nudging ethically and transparently. It is essential to ensure that nudges are in the best interest of clients and respect their autonomy. Here are some further considerations when applying behavioral economics and nudging in consulting:

A. *Ethical considerations:* Consultants must adhere to ethical guidelines when implementing nudges. It is crucial to ensure transparency and inform clients about the nudges being used, allowing them to opt out if they so choose. Respecting client autonomy and promoting informed decision-making should always be the guiding principles.

B. *Customization and context:* Nudges should be tailored to the specific needs, preferences, and context of each client. What works for one organization or individual may not be effective for another. Consultants should take into account the unique circumstances and characteristics of their clients when designing nudges to maximize their impact.

C. *Experimentation and evaluation:* Nudging strategies should be continually evaluated and refined based on real-world feedback. Consultants can conduct experiments to test the effectiveness of different nudges and adjust their approach accordingly. By collecting data and analyzing outcomes, consultants can refine their strategies and optimize results.

D. *Collaboration and buy-in:* Successful nudging requires collaboration and buy-in from key stakeholders within the client organization. Consultants should engage with decision-makers, executives, and employees to ensure that nudges are well-received and understood. Building support and enthusiasm for nudging initiatives can increase their effectiveness and sustainability.

E. *Long-term impact:* Nudges should not be viewed as quick fixes but as part of a broader change management strategy. Consultants should consider the long-term impact of nudging on organizational culture, employee behavior, and client outcomes. By incorporating nudging into a comprehensive approach, consultants can drive lasting behavioral change.

F. *Continuous learning:* Behavioral economics is a dynamic field, and new insights and research emerge regularly. Consultants should stay abreast of the latest developments, theories, and findings in behavioral economics to enhance their understanding and refine their nudging strategies. Continuous learning ensures that consultants can provide the most up-to-date and effective guidance to their clients.

In conclusion, behavioral economics and nudging offer valuable tools for consultants to influence decision-making and drive positive outcomes. By understanding cognitive biases, leveraging framing techniques, and designing choice architectures, consultants can nudge clients toward making choices that align with their goals and aspirations. However, it is essential to approach nudging ethically, respecting client autonomy, and ensuring transparency. With careful consideration, customization, and collaboration, consultants can harness the power of behavioral economics to shape decision-making in ways that drive success and deliver long-term benefits for their clients.

2.10 Communication and Active Listening

Effective communication is a fundamental skill in consulting that lays the groundwork for successful client engagements and the achievement of desired outcomes. Consultants must be adept at not only conveying information but also actively listening to clients and understanding their perspectives. This entails engaging in a dynamic and empathetic dialogue that fosters trust, collaboration, and mutual understanding. In this section, we will explore the importance of communication and active listening in consulting and provide practical strategies for consultants to enhance their communication skills.

Communication forms the foundation of a consultant–client relationship. Consultants should strive to establish rapport and build trust from the outset. This involves creating an open and welcoming environment, actively listening to clients' concerns, and demonstrating empathy and understanding. By cultivating a trusting relationship, consultants can foster collaboration and establish a strong foundation for effective communication.

Active listening is a critical component of effective communication. It involves not only hearing what clients say but also comprehending their message, understanding their emotions, and observing nonverbal cues. Consultants should practice active listening by maintaining eye contact, nodding to show understanding, and asking clarifying questions to ensure they fully grasp the client's perspective. By actively listening, consultants can gain valuable insights and demonstrate their commitment to understanding the client's needs.

Empathy plays a pivotal role in effective communication. It involves understanding and sharing the emotions and experiences of clients. Consultants should strive to communicate empathy by acknowledging clients' feelings, validating their concerns, and demonstrating genuine care and understanding. Empathetic communication fosters trust, strengthens relationships, and enhances the consultant's ability to provide meaningful support and guidance.

Consultants often deal with complex information and concepts. It is essential to convey these ideas in a clear and concise manner to ensure effective communication. Consultants should avoid jargon and technical language, instead opting for plain language that is easily understandable by clients. The use of visual aids, such as charts and diagrams, can also enhance clarity and facilitate comprehension.

Consultants interact with individuals at various levels within client organizations, each with their own roles, responsibilities, and areas of expertise. Effective communication involves tailoring the message and delivery to suit the specific audience. Consultants should consider the background knowledge, communication preferences, and priorities of the individuals they are communicating with. Adapting the communication style to the audience ensures that the message is received and understood effectively.

In consulting, consultants may encounter difficult conversations that involve addressing sensitive or contentious issues. Effective communication in such situations requires tact, diplomacy, and the ability to manage emotions. Consultants should approach difficult conversations with empathy, active listening, and an open-minded attitude. They should seek to understand the underlying concerns, address them directly, and work collaboratively with clients to find mutually agreeable solutions.

Nonverbal cues, such as body language, facial expressions, and tone of voice, play a significant role in communication. Consultants should be mindful of their own nonverbal cues and observe those of their clients. Maintaining an open posture, making eye contact, and using appropriate facial expressions and gestures can convey attentiveness and engagement. Similarly, interpreting clients' nonverbal cues can provide insights into their thoughts and emotions, facilitating a deeper understanding of their perspectives.

Effective communication is a two-way process. Consultants should actively seek feedback from clients to ensure that their messages are being received and understood as intended. This involves inviting clients to ask questions, seeking clarification on their understanding, and encouraging open dialogue. By actively seeking feedback, consultants can address any misunderstandings, refine their communication approach, and demonstrate their commitment to continuous improvement.

In today's globalized world, consultants often work with clients from diverse cultural backgrounds. Effective communication requires sensitivity and adaptability to cultural differences. Consultants should familiarize themselves with the cultural norms, communication styles, and expectations of their clients to ensure effective cross-cultural communication. This may involve adjusting communication strategies, being mindful of different communication preferences, and avoiding cultural misunderstandings.

Effective communication involves clarifying expectations and managing assumptions. Consultants should proactively communicate project objectives, timelines, deliverables, and the roles and responsibilities of both parties. By aligning expectations from the beginning, consultants can mitigate misunderstandings, ensure a shared understanding of project scope, and promote transparency and accountability.

In the digital age, consultants often communicate with clients through various technological platforms and mediums. It is crucial to select the most appropriate tools and channels for effective communication. Consultants should consider the nature of the message, the urgency of the communication, and the preferences of the clients. Whether it is face-to-face meetings, phone calls, video conferences, or email exchanges, choosing the right medium can enhance the efficiency and effectiveness of communication.

During consulting engagements, numerous discussions, decisions, and action items may arise. It is essential to document and summarize key discussions to ensure clarity, alignment, and accountability. Consultants should provide meeting minutes, action plans, and progress reports to clients, enabling them to review and reference important information. This documentation not only facilitates effective communication but also serves as a valuable reference for future engagements.

Effective communication is a skill that can be honed and refined over time. Consultants should engage in continuous learning and improvement by seeking feedback, reflecting on their communication experiences, and incorporating new strategies and techniques. Professional development opportunities, such as workshops, seminars, and coaching, can further enhance communication skills and ensure consultants stay current with best practices.

Effective communication and active listening are essential components of successful consulting engagements. By establishing rapport, practicing active listening, communicating empathy, and adapting to diverse audiences and cultural contexts, consultants can foster trust, collaboration, and understanding. Clear and concise communication, along with the ability to manage difficult conversations and seek feedback, enhances the consultant–client relationship and facilitates the achievement of desired outcomes. By continuously refining their communication skills and leveraging appropriate technology, consultants can navigate complex consulting projects with confidence and drive positive results for their clients.

2.11   Cross-Cultural Considerations

Cross-cultural considerations are of paramount importance in today's globalized world, where consultants often find themselves working with clients from diverse cultural backgrounds. In the field of consulting, understanding and navigating cultural differences is essential for building effective relationships, fostering collaboration, and achieving successful outcomes. When engaging with clients from different cultures, consultants must approach their interactions with sensitivity, respect, and open-mindedness.

They should recognize that cultural norms, values, communication styles, and expectations vary significantly across different societies. By embracing cultural diversity and considering these nuances, consultants can enhance their effectiveness and ensure their recommendations and strategies align with the unique needs and contexts of their clients. One of the key aspects of cross-cultural considerations is communication.

Consultants must recognize that communication styles can vary significantly across cultures. Direct and assertive communication may be valued in some cultures, while others may prioritize indirect and implicit communication. Understanding these differences allows consultants to adapt their communication approach accordingly. They must be mindful of language barriers, idiomatic expressions, and nonverbal cues, as misinterpretations can easily occur.

It is crucial to avoid assumptions and to seek clarification when needed, ensuring a shared understanding of ideas, objectives, and expectations. Another vital aspect is cultural values. Every culture has its own set of values, which influence decision-making, priorities, and approaches to problem-solving. Consultants should familiarize themselves with the cultural values of their clients to better understand their perspectives and decision-making processes. For example, individualistic cultures may prioritize personal achievement and independence, while collectivistic cultures may emphasize group harmony and consensus. Consultants need to adapt their strategies and recommendations accordingly, considering the cultural values that underpin their clients' organizations.

Cultural context also plays a significant role in consulting engagements. Consultants must take into account the political, economic, and social factors that shape the environment in which their clients operate. Laws, regulations, and business practices can differ significantly across countries, requiring consultants to navigate these complexities to provide effective guidance. Understanding the historical and social context of a culture can shed light on underlying motivations, power dynamics, and decision-making processes.

Consultants must be sensitive to cultural nuances and navigate the cultural context with finesse, ensuring their recommendations align with the realities and constraints of the clients' environment. Building relationships and establishing trust is another critical aspect of cross-cultural considerations. Trust is the foundation of successful consulting engagements, and it can take time to develop, particularly in cross-cultural settings.

Consultants should invest in building personal connections, demonstrating respect for local customs and traditions, and actively seeking to understand their clients' perspectives. This includes being aware of etiquette, greetings, and appropriate forms of address. By showing genuine interest in the culture and actively engaging with clients on a personal level, consultants can foster trust and create a conducive environment for collaboration.

Cross-cultural considerations also extend to decision-making processes. Consultants must be aware of how decisions are made within different cultural contexts. Some cultures have a hierarchical decision-making structure, where decisions are made by senior leaders, while others emphasize consensus-building and group involvement. Consultants should adapt their approach to fit the decision-making processes of their clients, ensuring that recommendations are presented in a manner that resonates with the cultural norms and expectations.

Additionally, consultants must be conscious of cultural differences in perception of time and deadlines. Some cultures prioritize punctuality and adhere strictly to timelines, while others have a more flexible approach to time. Consultants should manage their own expectations and adapt their project timelines and deadlines accordingly, taking into account the cultural perspectives on time. It is crucial to set realistic expectations and maintain clear communication regarding project timelines to avoid misunderstandings and frustrations. Lastly, consultants should embrace cultural learning and humility.

Recognizing that they may not have all the answers or fully understand the nuances of every culture is essential. Consultants should approach cross-cultural engagements with a willingness to learn, adapt, and acknowledge their own cultural biases and limitations.

They should actively seek to expand their cultural competence through education, training, and exposure to different cultures. This includes learning about the history, traditions, and customs of the cultures they engage with, as well as staying informed about current events and trends.

Consultants should also be open to feedback and be willing to course-correct if their actions or recommendations inadvertently offend or disregard cultural sensitivities. They should be receptive to input from their clients and be willing to modify their approach to better align with the cultural context.In addition to individual efforts, organizations can support cross-cultural considerations by fostering a diverse and inclusive work environment. By promoting diversity at all levels of the consulting firm, organizations can benefit from a broader range of perspectives and experiences. This diversity can contribute to a deeper understanding of cultural nuances and help consultants navigate cross-cultural engagements more effectively.

To address cross-cultural considerations in consulting engagements, organizations can establish internal guidelines or frameworks that promote cultural awareness and sensitivity. This may include providing consultants with resources, training programs, and access to cultural consultants who can offer insights and guidance specific to different cultures. Such initiatives can enable consultants to approach cross-cultural engagements with greater confidence and competence.

Moreover, partnerships with local experts or consultants who possess deep cultural knowledge can be valuable in bridging the cultural gap and facilitating effective communication and collaboration. These experts can provide invaluable insights into the cultural intricacies, unwritten rules, and expectations that may impact the success of the consulting engagement. Ultimately, effective cross-cultural considerations in consulting require a commitment to continuous learning, adaptation, and cultural intelligence. By valuing and respecting cultural differences, actively listening, and embracing diversity, consultants can build trust, foster collaboration, and deliver meaningful results for their clients in cross-cultural settings. In conclusion, cross-cultural considerations are vital for successful consulting engagements in today's globalized world.

Effective communication, understanding cultural values, recognizing cultural context, building relationships based on trust, adapting decision-making processes, and embracing cultural learning and humility are key elements in navigating cross-cultural engagements.

By incorporating these considerations into their consulting practice, consultants can bridge cultural gaps, foster effective communication, and provide tailored solutions that align with their clients' cultural context. Embracing cultural diversity not only enhances the outcomes of consulting engagements but also contributes to the growth and development of consultants and their organizations in an increasingly interconnected world.

2.12   Conflict Resolution and Negotiation

Conflict resolution and negotiation are integral skills for consultants working in dynamic and complex environments. In the realm of consulting, conflicts can arise due to differing perspectives, goals, interests, and expectations between stakeholders. Effective conflict resolution and negotiation strategies enable consultants to address these conflicts, find mutually beneficial solutions, and maintain positive working relationships with their clients. Conflict resolution involves managing and resolving disagreements or disputes that may arise during the consulting process. It is essential for consultants to approach conflicts with a proactive and constructive mindset, seeking to understand the underlying causes and finding ways to address them effectively.

By navigating conflicts skillfully, consultants can not only resolve immediate issues but also create opportunities for growth, collaboration, and innovation. One of the first steps in conflict resolution is to establish open lines of communication.

Consultants should encourage all parties involved to express their concerns, perspectives, and interests openly and respectfully.

Actively listening to all stakeholders is critical, as it helps consultants gain a deeper understanding of the underlying issues and emotions driving the conflict. By demonstrating empathy and acknowledging the validity of different viewpoints, consultants can create an atmosphere of trust and openness, which is crucial for successful conflict resolution. During the conflict resolution process, consultants should aim to identify common ground and shared objectives. By highlighting shared interests and goals, consultants can shift the focus from individual positions to a collaborative problem-solving mindset.

This approach helps stakeholders recognize that working together toward a mutually beneficial solution is in their best interest. Consultants can facilitate this process by reframing the conflict as an opportunity for joint problem-solving and emphasizing the potential positive outcomes that can result from resolving the conflict. Negotiation is a key component of conflict resolution, as it involves finding mutually acceptable solutions to the identified issues. Effective negotiation requires a combination of analytical thinking, creativity, and strong interpersonal skills. Consultants should be prepared to engage in principled negotiation, which involves focusing on interests, generating options, and seeking win-win solutions.

They should be adept at identifying underlying needs and interests of all parties involved and finding creative solutions that satisfy those needs. To negotiate successfully, consultants must be skilled in effective communication and persuasive techniques. They should clearly articulate their own position while also actively listening to the concerns and interests of other stakeholders. Active listening allows consultants to gain insights into the underlying needs and motivations of each party, facilitating the development of innovative and mutually beneficial solutions.

By demonstrating respect and understanding, consultants can build rapport and trust, which can significantly influence the outcome of negotiations. Another important aspect of negotiation is the ability to manage emotions and handle conflicts constructively. Consultants should remain calm, composed, and professional, even in the face of tense or emotional situations. Emotions can escalate conflicts and hinder productive negotiations, so consultants must strive to create a positive and supportive environment that encourages constructive dialogue.

They should also be skilled in managing potential power imbalances and ensuring that all parties feel heard and valued throughout the negotiation process. In some cases, consultants may encounter particularly challenging or entrenched conflicts. These conflicts may require additional strategies, such as mediation or facilitation. In such situations, consultants can play the role of a neutral third party who facilitates the discussion and guides stakeholders toward finding common ground.

Mediation and facilitation techniques help manage conflicts by providing a structured and neutral space for open dialogue, brainstorming solutions, and fostering understanding between parties.

Conflict resolution and negotiation skills are not only applicable during moments of tension or disagreement but can also be used proactively to prevent conflicts from escalating. Consultants can employ strategies such as clear communication, stakeholder engagement, and proactive problem-solving to anticipate and address potential conflicts before they arise. By promoting open communication channels and maintaining strong relationships with stakeholders, consultants can create an environment conducive to early conflict detection and resolution.

2.13 Ethical Considerations

Ethical considerations are of paramount importance in the field of consulting. As consultants engage with clients and provide professional advice, they must uphold ethical principles to ensure integrity, trustworthiness, and responsible decision-making. Ethical conduct is not only crucial for maintaining the reputation and credibility of consultants and consulting firms but also for safeguarding the best interests of clients and stakeholders.

One of the key ethical considerations in consulting is maintaining confidentiality. Consultants often have access to sensitive information about their clients' businesses, strategies, and operations. It is imperative that consultants respect and protect the confidentiality of this information. This includes safeguarding client data, trade secrets, and proprietary information from unauthorized disclosure or misuse. Consultants must follow established protocols and legal requirements regarding the handling and storage of confidential information.

By maintaining strict confidentiality, consultants demonstrate professionalism and build trust with their clients, fostering a collaborative and open working relationship. Conflicts of interest are another important ethical consideration in consulting. Consultants should be diligent in identifying and managing any potential conflicts of interest that may compromise their objectivity or impartiality.

This includes disclosing any relationships, financial interests, or personal biases that may influence their judgment or decision-making. By proactively addressing conflicts of interest, consultants can maintain the trust and confidence of their clients and ensure that their recommendations are driven by the best interests of the client rather than personal gain. Integrity and honesty are foundational ethical principles that consultants must adhere to.

Consultants should provide accurate and reliable information to clients, presenting findings and recommendations in an unbiased and transparent manner. It is essential to avoid misrepresentation, exaggeration, or withholding of information that may lead to false perceptions or misguided decisions. By upholding the highest standards of integrity, consultants demonstrate their commitment to ethical conduct and client welfare. In the consulting profession, independence is a critical ethical consideration. Consultants should strive to maintain independence in their judgment and decision-making processes.

This means avoiding undue influence, conflicts of interest, or any factors that may compromise objectivity. Independence ensures that consultants can provide impartial and unbiased advice, free from external pressures or personal interests. It is essential for consultants to exercise professional skepticism, critically evaluate information, and challenge assumptions to ensure the integrity and quality of their work. Ethical considerations in consulting also encompass the responsibility to provide accurate and realistic expectations to clients.

Consultants should set clear expectations about the scope, deliverables, timelines, and potential limitations of their services. This includes being transparent about the potential risks, challenges, and uncertainties associated with the proposed solutions. By setting realistic expectations, consultants promote trust and manage client's expectations, ensuring that clients have a clear understanding of what can be achieved and the potential outcomes of their engagement.

Informed consent is another ethical consideration that consultants should prioritize. Consultants must ensure that clients fully understand the nature of the consulting engagement, including the objectives, methodologies, and potential implications of the proposed recommendations. Consultants should communicate the potential benefits, risks, and limitations associated with the consulting process, empowering clients to make informed decisions.

By obtaining informed consent, consultants respect the autonomy and right of clients to participate in decision-making processes that affect their organizations. Furthermore, diversity and inclusion are vital ethical considerations in consulting. Consultants should strive to promote diversity and inclusivity in their interactions with clients and stakeholders. This includes valuing and respecting individual differences, avoiding discrimination, and promoting equal opportunities. Consultants should actively seek diverse perspectives, engage diverse stakeholders, and ensure that their recommendations consider the broader impact on all relevant stakeholders. By embracing diversity and inclusion, consultants foster innovation, creativity, and social responsibility in their consulting engagements.

Ethical considerations also extend to the responsibilities consultants have toward society and the broader community. Consultants should conduct their work with social and environmental awareness, taking into account the potential impact of their recommendations on stakeholders, communities, and the environment. This includes considering sustainability, ethical sourcing, social responsibility, and the long-term consequences of the proposed solutions.

Consultants should strive to create positive social impact and contribute to sustainable development through their work. This may involve integrating ethical and socially responsible practices into client operations, promoting corporate social responsibility initiatives, or offering guidance on environmentally friendly practices. Consultants must also be aware of the potential risks and ethical implications of emerging technologies and data privacy. With the increasing use of technology in consulting, consultants must be vigilant in protecting client data, ensuring compliance with relevant data protection regulations, and addressing any ethical concerns related to data privacy and security.

They should handle data with integrity and transparency, seeking informed consent and using data only for legitimate purposes. In addition to these specific ethical considerations, consultants should adhere to professional codes of conduct and industry standards. Professional organizations often establish guidelines and ethical frameworks that consultants should follow.

These codes typically outline principles such as integrity, confidentiality, objectivity, and competence, providing a foundation for ethical behavior in consulting. Consultants should familiarize themselves with these codes and apply them to their work.It is also important for consulting firms to establish a strong ethical culture within their organizations. This involves providing ethics training and education to consultants, promoting open discussions about ethical dilemmas, and fostering an environment that encourages ethical behavior.

Consulting firms should have mechanisms in place for consultants to seek guidance or report any ethical concerns confidentially. By creating an ethical culture, consulting firms can reinforce the importance of ethical conduct and empower consultants to make responsible decisions. In conclusion, ethical considerations play a crucial role in the consulting profession.

Consultants must prioritize confidentiality, manage conflicts of interest, maintain integrity and honesty, exercise independence and objectivity, provide realistic expectations, obtain informed consent, promote diversity and inclusion, and consider social and environmental impacts.

By upholding ethical principles, consultants build trust, preserve their professional reputation, and contribute to the overall welfare of their clients and society. Ethical conduct is not just a moral obligation but also a fundamental requirement for delivering high-quality consulting services that have a positive and lasting impact.

Chapter 3
Finding New Clients

Finding new clients is an essential part of being a successful business consultant. As a consultant, your job is to help businesses solve problems and improve their operations. But in order to do that, you need clients to work with. Finding new clients can be a challenge, but with the right strategies and techniques, it can be done effectively.

One of the first steps in finding new clients is to identify your target market. This means figuring out who your ideal clients are, what industries they are in, and what types of problems they need help with. Once you have a clear understanding of your target market, you can begin to develop marketing strategies to reach out to them.

Networking is also a key component of finding new clients. Attending industry events, conferences, and trade shows can be a great way to meet potential clients and introduce them to your services. You can also join professional associations and organizations related to your industry, which can provide you with opportunities to network with other professionals and potentially generate new business leads.

Another effective way to find new clients is through referrals. When you have satisfied clients, ask them to refer you to other businesses that may benefit from your services. You can also ask for testimonials or case studies that you can use to showcase your success with past clients.

In addition to networking and referrals, digital marketing can also be a powerful tool for finding new clients. This includes having a strong online presence with a professional website, active social media profiles, and search engine optimization (SEO) strategies to improve your visibility in online search results.

Cold outreach is another way to find new clients, but it requires a targeted approach. This means researching potential clients and reaching out to them with a personalized message that highlights how your services can help them solve specific problems or achieve their goals. This approach can be effective, but it requires a significant amount of research and effort.

Once you have identified potential clients and have established communication with them, it's important to approach the relationship in a professional and strategic

© The Author(s), under exclusive license to Springer Nature Switzerland AG 2023   43
F. Addimando, *Client-Centered Business Consulting*, SpringerBriefs in
Psychology, https://doi.org/10.1007/978-3-031-42844-9_3

way. This means understanding their needs and goals, and tailoring your services and approach to meet those needs.

Communication is key in maintaining relationships with clients. This means keeping them updated on progress, responding promptly to their questions and concerns, and providing regular updates and reports. It's also important to be transparent and honest about your services and what you can realistically achieve for them.

In conclusion, finding new clients is an essential part of being a successful business consultant. It requires a strategic approach that includes identifying your target market, networking, referrals, digital marketing, and targeted outreach. Once you have established communication with potential clients, it's important to approach the relationship in a professional and strategic way and to maintain strong communication and transparency throughout the engagement. With these strategies in place, you can effectively find new clients and grow your business as a consultant.

3.1   Identifying Potential Clients

In the world of business consulting, identifying potential clients is a crucial step in growing your business and expanding your network. It involves the process of identifying individuals or organizations that have a need for your consulting services and could potentially become your clients. This is an important step in the business consulting process as it sets the foundation for your outreach and marketing strategies.

There are several methods for identifying potential clients in the business consulting industry. The first step is to define your target market. This involves identifying the specific industry or niche that you specialize in, as well as the types of clients that would benefit from your services. Once you have identified your target market, you can then begin to identify potential clients within that market.

One effective method for identifying potential clients is through networking. Attending industry events, conferences, and trade shows can help you connect with potential clients and establish new business relationships. You can also leverage your existing network by asking for referrals and introductions to individuals or organizations that may benefit from your services.

Another method for identifying potential clients is through research. This involves conducting market research to identify potential clients who may have a need for your services. This can include analyzing industry trends, studying the competition, and conducting surveys or focus groups to gather feedback from potential clients.

In addition to networking and research, it is also important to develop a strong online presence. This includes creating a professional website and social media profiles that showcase your expertise and services. Utilizing search engine optimization (SEO) strategies can also help potential clients find you online when searching for consulting services in your niche or industry.

Once you have identified potential clients, the next step is to prioritize them based on their level of interest and need for your services. This can be done through a process known as lead scoring, which involves assigning points or rankings to potential clients based on their level of engagement and potential to become a paying client.

It is also important to tailor your outreach and marketing strategies to the needs and preferences of potential clients. This can include personalizing your communication and messaging to speak directly to their pain points and challenges, as well as offering customized solutions and proposals that meet their specific needs.

In addition to identifying potential clients, it is also important to maintain a database or CRM (customer relationship management) system to track your interactions and progress with each potential client. This can help you stay organized and informed, as well as provide valuable insights and data to inform your future outreach and marketing strategies.

In conclusion, identifying potential clients is a critical step in growing your business as a business consultant. By defining your target market, leveraging your network, conducting research, developing a strong online presence, and prioritizing leads, you can effectively identify potential clients and establish new business relationships. By tailoring your outreach and marketing strategies to the needs and preferences of potential clients, you can increase your chances of converting leads into paying clients and building a successful consulting business.

3.2 Developing a Marketing Strategy

Developing a marketing strategy is crucial for business consulting firms that aim to acquire and retain clients. A well-designed marketing strategy can help consulting firms differentiate themselves from competitors and effectively communicate their value proposition to potential clients. In this section, we will discuss the key steps involved in developing a marketing strategy for business consulting firms.

3.2.1 Step 1: Define Your Target Market

Before developing a marketing strategy, it is important to identify the target market for the consulting firm's services. The target market may be defined by industry, company size, geography, or other factors. Once the target market has been defined, the consulting firm can begin to develop a marketing strategy that is tailored to the needs and preferences of that market.

3.2.2 Step 2: Understand the Competitive Landscape

In order to differentiate themselves from competitors, consulting firms must have a thorough understanding of the competitive landscape. This includes identifying the strengths and weaknesses of key competitors, as well as the types of services they offer and the pricing strategies they use. By understanding the competitive landscape, consulting firms can position themselves as a unique and valuable option for potential clients.

3.2.3 Step 3: Develop a Value Proposition

A value proposition is a statement that describes the unique value that a consulting firm can offer to its clients. It should be clear, concise, and differentiated from the value propositions of competitors. The value proposition should be developed based on a deep understanding of the target market and the problems that potential clients are trying to solve.

3.2.4 Step 4: Determine the Marketing Mix

The marketing mix refers to the set of tactics that a consulting firm will use to promote its services. These tactics may include advertising, public relations, direct marketing, events, and digital marketing. The marketing mix should be tailored to the needs and preferences of the target market, as well as the firm's budget and resources.

3.2.5 Step 5: Establish Metrics and KPIs

In order to measure the success of the marketing strategy, consulting firms must establish metrics and key performance indicators (KPIs). These may include metrics such as website traffic, social media engagement, and lead generation. By tracking these metrics, consulting firms can identify areas where the marketing strategy is working well and areas where it may need to be adjusted.

3.2.6   Step 6: Implement and Monitor the Marketing Strategy

Once the marketing strategy has been developed, it must be implemented and moni-tored to ensure that it is effective. This may involve working with advertising agen-cies or other marketing professionals to execute the tactics outlined in the marketing mix. It is important to monitor the results of the marketing strategy on an ongoing basis and make adjustments as needed to ensure that it is achieving its objectives.

In conclusion, developing a marketing strategy is critical for business consulting firms that want to acquire and retain clients. By defining the target market, under-standing the competitive landscape, developing a value proposition, determining the marketing mix, establishing metrics and KPIs, and implementing and monitoring the marketing strategy, consulting firms can effectively communicate their value proposition to potential clients and differentiate themselves from competitors.

3.3   Cold Calling and Email Outreach

Cold calling and email outreach are two common methods used by business consul-tants to reach out to potential clients. While these methods may seem outdated in today's digital age, they can still be effective if used correctly.

Cold calling involves making unsolicited phone calls to potential clients in the hopes of generating interest in your consulting services. Email outreach, on the other hand, involves sending targeted emails to potential clients to introduce your-self and your services.

While both methods can be effective, they require a well-planned and well-executed strategy to be successful. In this section, we'll explore the best practices for cold calling and email outreach in the context of business consulting.

3.3.1   Cold Calling

Cold calling can be an effective way to generate leads for your business consulting services. However, it's important to approach it strategically in order to maximize your chances of success.

3.3.1.1   Research Your Prospects

Before making any cold calls, it's important to do your research on the prospects you'll be calling. This includes understanding their industry, business model, pain points, and potential needs for consulting services. By doing this, you'll be better equipped to tailor your pitch and offer value to the prospect.

3.3.1.2   Prepare a Script

While you don't want to sound like a robot on the phone, it's important to prepare a script to guide your conversation. This should include an introduction, a brief explanation of your services, and a call-to-action for the prospect to learn more.

3.3.1.3   Practice Your Pitch

Practice makes perfect, and this is especially true when it comes to cold calling. Take the time to practice your pitch until it flows naturally and you're comfortable with the conversation.

3.3.1.4   Make the Call

When it's time to make the call, be sure to introduce yourself and ask if it's a good time to talk. Respect the prospect's time and be concise in your pitch. If they express interest, be prepared to answer their questions and set up a follow-up conversation.

3.3.1.5   Follow Up

Following up is crucial in cold calling. If you don't hear back from a prospect after your initial call, don't give up. Send a follow-up email or call again at a later time to keep the conversation going.

3.3.2   Email Outreach

Email outreach can be a less intrusive way to reach potential clients and introduce your consulting services. However, like cold calling, it requires a strategic approach to be effective.

3.3.2.1   Build a Targeted List

The first step in email outreach is building a targeted list of prospects who may be interested in your services. This can be done through research and networking or by purchasing a targeted list from a reputable provider.

3.3.2.2 Craft a Compelling Subject Line

Your email subject line is the first thing a prospect will see, so it's important to make it compelling. A clear and concise subject line that offers value to the recipient is more likely to be opened.

3.3.2.3 Personalize Your Message

Personalization is key in email outreach. Address the recipient by name, and tailor your message to their specific needs and pain points.

3.3.2.4 Offer Value

In your email, offer value to the recipient by highlighting how your consulting services can help them solve their business challenges. Be specific and provide examples of your past successes.

3.3.2.5 Include a Call-to-Action

Finally, be sure to include a clear call-to-action in your email. This can be as simple as asking the recipient to schedule a call with you to learn more about your services.

In conclusion, while cold calling and email outreach may seem outdated, they can still be effective methods for reaching potential clients as a business consultant. By following the best practices outlined in this chapter, you can increase your chances of success and generate more leads for your consulting services.

3.4 Networking Events and Conferences

Networking events and conferences are a great way for business consultants to meet potential clients, build their brand, and learn about industry trends. These events provide opportunities to make connections with other professionals, exchange ideas and information, and promote services. In this section, we will explore how networking events and conferences can be beneficial for business consultants, how to prepare for them, and how to make the most of these opportunities.

3.4.1 Why Attend Networking Events and Conferences?

Networking events and conferences are an important aspect of building a successful business consulting practice. By attending these events, consultants can:

- Meet Potential Clients: Networking events and conferences provide an opportunity to meet potential clients face-to-face. This can be much more effective than cold calling or emailing because it allows consultants to build a personal relationship with prospects.
- Learn About Industry Trends: Conferences and networking events are also a great way to learn about the latest trends and developments in the industry. Consultants can attend presentations and workshops to gain insights into new techniques and best practices, which they can then apply to their consulting practice.
- Build Relationships with Other Professionals: Networking events and conferences provide an opportunity to build relationships with other professionals in the industry. This can lead to future referrals and collaborations, as well as access to new resources and information.
- Promote Services: Finally, networking events and conferences are a great way to promote services and build brand awareness. By meeting potential clients and other professionals, consultants can raise awareness of their services and differentiate themselves from competitors.

3.4.2 Preparing for Networking Events and Conferences

To make the most of networking events and conferences, it's important to prepare in advance. Here are some tips for preparing:

- Identify Goals: Before attending an event, identify your goals. What do you hope to achieve by attending? Are you looking to meet potential clients, learn about new trends and best practices, or promote your services?
- Research Attendees: Review the attendee list and research the individuals and companies you want to meet. This will help you tailor your conversations and approach to their needs and interests.
- Prepare Your Elevator Pitch: Develop a clear and concise elevator pitch that explains who you are, what you do, and the value you bring to clients. Practice it until you can deliver it confidently.
- Bring Business Cards: Bring plenty of business cards to hand out to potential clients and other professionals you meet. Make sure your cards include your contact information, website, and social media profiles.
- Dress Appropriately: Dress professionally and appropriately for the event. First impressions matter, and your appearance can impact how others perceive you.

3.4.3 Making the Most of Networking Events and Conferences

Once you arrive at a networking event or conference, it's important to make the most of the opportunity. Here are some tips for maximizing your time:

- Be Proactive: Don't wait for people to approach you. Take the initiative to introduce yourself to others and start conversations.
- Listen More Than You Talk: When you meet someone, listen to what they have to say. Ask questions and show interest in their business and goals. This will help you build a rapport and establish a relationship.
- Follow Up: After the event, follow up with the people you met. Send an email or LinkedIn message thanking them for their time and suggesting a follow-up call or meeting.
- Be Patient: Building relationships takes time. Don't expect to walk away from a networking event with a new client or project. Instead, focus on building long-term relationships that can lead to future opportunities.
- Stay in Touch: Finally, stay in touch with the people you meet. Connect with them on social media, share relevant content, and keep them updated on your services and successes. This will help you stay top of mind and increase the likelihood of future collaborations.

3.5 Leveraging Social Media

In today's digital age, social media has become an essential tool for business growth and development. It provides a platform for businesses to connect with their customers, build brand awareness, and generate new leads. As a business consultant, leveraging social media can be a powerful way to establish a strong online presence and expand your client base.

In this section, we will discuss how business consultants can effectively leverage social media to promote their services and engage with potential clients.

3.5.1 Establish Your Presence on Social Media

The first step to leveraging social media as a business consultant is to establish your presence on the major social media platforms. This includes creating profiles on LinkedIn, Twitter, Facebook, and Instagram. These platforms offer unique benefits that can help you reach your target audience and build your brand.

LinkedIn, for example, is a professional networking site where you can connect with other professionals and showcase your expertise. Twitter allows you to engage with potential clients in real-time and share industry news and insights. Facebook and Instagram are great for building brand awareness and showcasing your personality and company culture.

3.5.2   Create Quality Content

Once you have established your presence on social media, the next step is to create quality content that will engage your audience. This can include blog posts, articles, infographics, and videos. Your content should be informative, engaging, and relevant to your target audience.

When creating content, it is important to keep in mind that social media users have short attention spans. Therefore, your content should be visually appealing, easy to read, and formatted for easy consumption.

3.5.3   Engage with Your Audience

Social media is a two-way street, and it is essential to engage with your audience to build relationships and establish trust. This can involve responding to comments, sharing and liking posts, and participating in industry discussions.

Engaging with your audience can also help you identify potential clients and generate leads. By actively participating in industry discussions and offering your expertise, you can position yourself as a thought leader in your field and attract new clients.

3.5.4   Utilize Social Media Advertising

Social media advertising can be a powerful tool for reaching your target audience and generating new leads. Platforms like Facebook and LinkedIn offer sophisticated targeting options that allow you to reach users based on factors like job title, company size, and industry.

Social media advertising can be especially effective when combined with other marketing strategies like email outreach and content marketing. By promoting your content and services through social media advertising, you can increase your visibility and generate new leads.

3.5.5 *Monitor Your Results*

Finally, it is essential to monitor your social media results to determine what is working and what is not. This can involve tracking your engagement metrics like likes, shares, and comments, as well as monitoring your website traffic and lead generation efforts.

By monitoring your results, you can adjust your social media strategy to maximize your results and improve your ROI. This may involve tweaking your content, adjusting your targeting options, or experimenting with new ad formats.

In conclusion, social media is a powerful tool for business consultants to establish a strong online presence, engage with potential clients, and generate new leads. By following these best practices, you can leverage social media to expand your client base and grow your business.

4.5.5. Monitor Your Results

Chapter 4
Approaching the Client

Approaching the client is a critical aspect of business consulting, and it can make or break the success of a consultant–client engagement. The initial approach sets the tone for the entire relationship and influences the client's willingness to share information, collaborate, and engage with the consultant's advice. As such, it is essential to approach clients in a way that inspires confidence, builds trust, and showcases the consultant's value proposition.

The first step in approaching the client is to research their organization, industry, competition, and business challenges. This research provides a foundation for understanding the client's needs, goals, and constraints, which are essential for developing an approach that aligns with their objectives. The consultant can use various sources of information, such as company websites, annual reports, press releases, industry publications, and social media, to gather data and insights.

Once the consultant has sufficient information about the client, they can develop an approach that reflects their understanding of the client's needs and challenges. The approach should be tailored to the client's business and objectives, and it should demonstrate the consultant's expertise and value proposition. It is crucial to avoid a one-size-fits-all approach, as it can undermine the consultant's credibility and damage the relationship.

The next step is to initiate contact with the client, which can be done through various channels, such as email, phone, or social media. The consultant should choose a channel that aligns with the client's preferences and is professional and respectful. In the initial contact, the consultant should introduce themselves, explain their expertise and experience, and express their interest in working with the client.

The consultant should also seek to understand the client's perspective and engage in a conversation that demonstrates their expertise and ability to add value. The consultant should listen actively, ask open-ended questions, and clarify their understanding of the client's needs and objectives. This approach builds rapport and trust and sets the stage for a productive engagement.

© The Author(s), under exclusive license to Springer Nature Switzerland AG 2023   55
F. Addimando, *Client-Centered Business Consulting*, SpringerBriefs in
Psychology, https://doi.org/10.1007/978-3-031-42844-9_4

It is essential to be respectful of the client's time and schedule, and to avoid being too aggressive or pushy in the initial approach. The consultant should seek to establish a relationship based on mutual respect and trust and work collaboratively with the client to achieve their objectives.

During the initial approach, the consultant should also be transparent about their fees and billing structure and provide the client with a clear understanding of what they can expect in terms of deliverables, timelines, and outcomes. The consultant should also be open to negotiation and flexible in their approach, as different clients have different needs and preferences.

Another critical aspect of approaching the client is to follow up and maintain regular communication. Following up after the initial contact demonstrates the consultant's commitment to the relationship and helps to keep the engagement on track. Regular communication can be done through various channels, such as email, phone, or in-person meetings, and should be tailored to the client's preferences.

In conclusion, approaching the client is a critical aspect of business consulting, and it requires a strategic and tailored approach. The consultant should research the client's organization and industry, develop an approach that aligns with their objectives, initiate contact through a professional and respectful channel, engage in a conversation that demonstrates their expertise and value proposition, be transparent about fees and billing structure, and maintain regular communication. By following these steps, the consultant can build a relationship based on mutual respect and trust and deliver value to the client.

4.1 Preparing for the First Meeting

Preparing for the first meeting with a potential client is one of the most critical steps in business consulting. It's an opportunity to make a good first impression and establish credibility. Proper preparation can make the difference between winning or losing a client, and it sets the tone for the entire consulting engagement. In this section, we will discuss the essential steps to take when preparing for the first meeting.

4.1.1 Research the Client

Before you meet with a potential client, it's essential to research their business thoroughly. This research should include learning about the company's history, the products or services they offer, their target market, and their competitors. The more you know about the company, the better you can understand their needs and develop a customized proposal.

You should also research the industry to gain a broader understanding of the client's business environment. This knowledge will help you identify trends and opportunities that could be leveraged to the client's advantage. By demonstrating an understanding of the industry, you show that you are a knowledgeable and competent consultant.

4.1.2 Understand the Client's Needs

During your research, it's important to identify the client's needs. What challenges are they facing? What goals do they want to achieve? What is their budget for consulting services? Understanding the client's needs is essential to develop a customized proposal that meets their requirements.

To identify the client's needs, you may need to conduct interviews with key stakeholders in the company, review financial statements, and analyze market data. The goal is to gain a thorough understanding of the client's business and the problems they are facing. This information will help you develop a proposal that addresses their needs and demonstrates your expertise.

4.1.3 Prepare a Customized Proposal

Based on your research, you should prepare a customized proposal that outlines your proposed consulting services. The proposal should demonstrate how you will help the client achieve their goals and solve their problems. It should be clear, concise, and tailored to the client's specific needs.

The proposal should also include your approach to the engagement, your methodology, and your deliverables. It should provide a timeline and budget for the project, as well as any relevant experience or references. A well-crafted proposal demonstrates your professionalism and sets the stage for a successful consulting engagement.

4.1.4 Establish Communication Protocol

Another critical step in preparing for the first meeting is to establish a communication protocol. It's essential to determine how you will communicate with the client during the engagement, and what the expectations are for response times and feedback.

You should also establish a process for managing project changes and updating the client on progress. By establishing clear communication protocols, you can avoid misunderstandings and ensure that both you and the client are on the same page throughout the engagement.

4.1.5   *Prepare Questions*

During the first meeting, you will have an opportunity to ask the client questions to gain a deeper understanding of their needs and goals. It's important to prepare questions in advance that will help you identify key areas of concern and opportunities for improvement.

Some sample questions to ask during the first meeting might include:

- What challenges are you currently facing in your business?
- What goals do you have for your business?
- What are your expectations for this consulting engagement?
- What metrics will be used to measure the success of the project?
- What are the budget constraints for this project?

By asking the right questions, you can gain a clear understanding of the client's needs and goals, and tailor your proposal to meet those requirements.

4.1.6   *Practice Your Presentation*

Finally, it's essential to practice your presentation in advance of the first meeting. Practice can help you refine your message, identify areas that need improvement, and build your confidence.

During your practice sessions, focus on your body language, tone of voice, and pace. Make sure that you are engaging and confident and that you project a professional image.

4.2   Conducting a Needs Analysis

Conducting a needs analysis is an essential step in the process of business consulting. It is a thorough examination of the client's business operations to identify areas where the consultant can provide support and make recommendations for improvement. This analysis involves gathering information and data about the client's business, which can include interviewing stakeholders, reviewing financial statements, and analyzing performance metrics. The ultimate goal is to understand the client's challenges and opportunities and provide tailored recommendations that can help the business achieve its goals.

One of the key benefits of conducting a needs analysis is that it allows the consultant to gain a deep understanding of the client's business. By asking questions and reviewing data, the consultant can identify areas where the business is struggling or underperforming. For example, the consultant may find that the client's sales team is not meeting their targets or that their production process is inefficient.

This insight allows the consultant to provide targeted recommendations that address specific problems and drive improvement.

The needs analysis process typically begins with an initial consultation between the consultant and the client. During this meeting, the consultant should aim to establish a rapport with the client and gather basic information about their business. This can include information about the company's history, its products or services, its competitors, and its target market. The consultant should also ask the client about their goals and objectives for the business, as well as any specific challenges they are facing.

Once the initial consultation is complete, the consultant will typically begin the process of gathering data and conducting research. This can involve reviewing financial statements and performance metrics, as well as conducting interviews with stakeholders such as employees, customers, and suppliers. The consultant may also conduct a SWOT analysis, which involves identifying the client's strengths, weaknesses, opportunities, and threats.

As the consultant conducts their research, they should keep in mind the client's goals and objectives. For example, if the client has expressed a desire to increase sales, the consultant should focus their analysis on identifying barriers to sales growth and opportunities to increase revenue. Similarly, if the client is concerned about operational efficiency, the consultant should look for ways to streamline processes and eliminate waste.

Once the data-gathering and analysis phase is complete, the consultant will typically prepare a report that summarizes their findings and provides recommendations for improvement. This report should be clear and concise and should focus on actionable steps that the client can take to achieve their goals. The consultant should also be prepared to present their findings to the client in a clear and engaging manner, using visual aids and other tools as necessary to help the client understand the information presented.

One of the key challenges of conducting a needs analysis is balancing the need for data and information with the need to establish rapport and build trust with the client. It is important for the consultant to be sensitive to the client's needs and concerns, and to be transparent about their process and the information they are gathering. This can help build trust and establish a positive working relationship between the consultant and the client.

In conclusion, conducting a needs analysis is a critical step in the process of business consulting. It allows the consultant to gain a deep understanding of the client's business and provide tailored recommendations that drive improvement and help the business achieve its goals. By asking questions, gathering data, and analyzing information, the consultant can identify areas for improvement and provide clear and actionable recommendations. The key to success is balancing the need for data and information with the need to build rapport and trust with the client, in order to establish a positive working relationship and drive meaningful results.

4.3   Demonstrating Your Expertise

As a business, it is important to demonstrate your expertise to potential clients. This not only helps to establish credibility but also builds trust, making it more likely that the client will choose to work with you. There are a number of ways to demonstrate your expertise, and this section will explore some of the most effective methods.

- Share your credentials: One of the most basic ways to demonstrate your expertise is to share your credentials. This could include your education, professional experience, certifications, and any awards or recognition you have received. Including this information on your website or in your marketing materials can help establish you as an expert in your field.
- Provide case studies: Another way to demonstrate your expertise is to provide case studies that showcase your skills and experience. Case studies can illustrate how you have helped clients in the past and provide tangible evidence of your abilities. Be sure to highlight specific results and outcomes that you have achieved for your clients.
- Share testimonials and references: Testimonials and references from satisfied clients can be a powerful tool for demonstrating your expertise. Ask your clients for permission to share their feedback and include these testimonials on your website or in your marketing materials. You may also want to offer references to potential clients who are considering working with you.
- Publish thought leadership content: Publishing thought leadership content, such as blog posts, white papers, and articles, can help to establish you as an expert in your field. This content should be informative and helpful to your target audience, providing insights and solutions to common problems. Publishing this content on your website or in industry publications can help to increase your visibility and credibility.
- Speak at industry events: Speaking at industry events, such as conferences and trade shows, is a great way to demonstrate your expertise and establish yourself as a thought leader. Look for opportunities to speak on panels, lead workshops, or deliver keynote addresses. This can help to increase your visibility and credibility in your field.
- Offer training and workshops: Offering training and workshops is another way to demonstrate your expertise and provide value to potential clients. These training sessions can be designed to address common challenges faced by your target audience and provide practical solutions. This can help to establish you as a trusted advisor and increase your chances of winning new business.
- Volunteer and contribute to your community: Volunteering and contributing to your community can also help to establish your expertise and build trust with potential clients. Look for opportunities to get involved with professional organizations, industry groups, and community organizations. This can help to increase your visibility and credibility in your field, while also providing opportunities to connect with potential clients.

In conclusion, demonstrating your expertise is critical to building trust and credibility with potential clients. By sharing your credentials, providing case studies and testimonials, publishing thought leadership content, speaking at industry events, offering training and workshops, and volunteering and contributing to your community, you can establish yourself as a trusted advisor and increase your chances of winning new business.

4.4 Addressing Concerns and Objections

In the world of business consulting, addressing concerns and objections is a critical component of building trust with clients and ensuring successful outcomes. It's common for clients to have questions, doubts, and reservations about the consulting process, and it's the consultant's job to identify these concerns and address them effectively. In this section, we'll explore the importance of addressing concerns and objections, how to identify them, and strategies for addressing them.

4.4.1 The Importance of Addressing Concerns and Objections

Addressing concerns and objections is essential because it helps build trust between the consultant and the client. It also helps the consultant to identify potential obstacles that could derail the consulting project. By addressing these concerns and objections upfront, the consultant can work to overcome them and build a stronger relationship with the client.

Clients may have concerns and objections about various aspects of the consulting process, including the consultant's expertise, the approach being used, the timeline and budget, and the potential outcomes. These concerns can range from minor doubts to significant reservations that may threaten to derail the project altogether. Addressing these concerns in a professional and effective manner can make all the difference between a successful engagement and a failed one.

4.4.2 Identifying Concerns and Objections

The first step in addressing concerns and objections is identifying them. This can be done in several ways, including:

- Listening carefully to the client's concerns during initial meetings and subsequent conversations.
- Asking questions to uncover any doubts or reservations that the client may have.

- Reviewing any written correspondence from the client to identify areas where they may be expressing concerns or objections.
- Observing the client's body language and tone of voice during conversations to identify any signs of hesitation or doubt.

Once the consultant has identified concerns and objections, they can begin to address them effectively.

4.4.3   Strategies for Addressing Concerns and Objections

- Acknowledge the concern or objection: The first step in addressing any concern or objection is to acknowledge it. The consultant should listen carefully to the client's concern and demonstrate that they understand the issue at hand.
- Provide evidence or data to support your position: Once the concern has been acknowledged, the consultant should provide evidence or data to support their position. This evidence could include case studies, research studies, or other forms of data that demonstrate the effectiveness of the consultant's approach.
- Offer alternative solutions: If the client's concern or objection is related to a specific aspect of the consulting process, the consultant should be prepared to offer alternative solutions. This could include adjusting the timeline, modifying the approach, or revising the budget.
- Address the root cause: If the client's concern or objection is related to a deeper issue, the consultant should work to address the root cause. This may involve additional research, gathering feedback from stakeholders, or modifying the project plan.
- Show empathy and understanding: Throughout the process of addressing concerns and objections, it's essential to show empathy and understanding to the client. The consultant should be patient, listen carefully, and demonstrate that they understand the client's perspective.
- Reassure the client: Finally, the consultant should reassure the client that their concerns have been heard and addressed. This can help to build trust and confidence in the consulting relationship.
- Addressing concerns and objections is a critical component of business consulting. It's essential to identify potential obstacles and work to address them proactively. By listening carefully, providing evidence and data, offering alternative solutions, addressing the root cause, showing empathy and understanding, and reassuring the client, consultants can build trust and confidence with their clients and ensure successful outcomes.

4.5   Securing the Engagement

Securing an engagement is one of the most crucial aspects of business consulting. After going through the initial stages of prospecting and qualifying a lead, demonstrating your expertise, and addressing their concerns and objections, the next step is to close the deal and secure the engagement. In this section, we'll delve into the different strategies you can use to secure an engagement.

4.5.1   Establishing Value

The first and foremost step in securing an engagement is to establish the value of your services. You need to demonstrate to the client how your services can help them achieve their goals and overcome the challenges they are facing. You need to show them the ROI of your services and how investing in your services will benefit their business in the long run. You can do this by presenting case studies of previous clients, outlining the services you can offer and the benefits they bring, and giving a clear and concise overview of your processes.

4.5.2   Proposal Development

Once you have established the value of your services, you need to develop a proposal that outlines your services and their pricing. You need to ensure that the proposal is customized to the specific needs of the client and highlights the benefits of your services. Your proposal should clearly outline the scope of the engagement, the timeline, the deliverables, and the costs involved.

4.5.3   Negotiating and Closing the Deal

After presenting the proposal, you will most likely receive feedback from the client, and they may have objections or concerns. You need to address these concerns and negotiate to find a mutually beneficial solution. It's essential to understand that negotiation is a give-and-take process, and you need to be flexible in your approach. Once both parties have agreed to the terms, you can close the deal and move onto the next phase of the engagement.

4.5.4 Setting Expectations

Before starting the engagement, it's crucial to set clear expectations with the client. You need to outline the roles and responsibilities of both parties, the timeline, and the deliverables. Setting expectations early on helps to prevent misunderstandings and ensures that both parties are on the same page. This is particularly important when working with difficult clients or on complex projects.

4.5.5 Contract Development

Once the engagement has been secured, you need to develop a contract that outlines the terms of the engagement. The contract should include the scope of the engagement, the timeline, the deliverables, the costs involved, and any other relevant terms and conditions. The contract should be clear, concise, and easy to understand and should be signed by both parties before starting the engagement.

4.5.6 Communication

Effective communication is key to a successful engagement. You need to maintain regular communication with the client throughout the engagement to ensure that everything is on track and that any issues or concerns are addressed promptly. Regular communication helps to build trust and ensures that both parties are working toward the same goals.

4.5.7 Managing Expectations

Managing expectations is crucial to maintaining a positive relationship with the client. You need to ensure that you deliver on your promises and meet the expectations set out in the contract. If issues arise during the engagement, you need to address them promptly and communicate any changes to the client. Managing expectations helps to build trust and ensures that the engagement is a success.

In conclusion, securing an engagement is a critical part of business consulting. It requires establishing the value of your services, developing a customized proposal, negotiating and closing the deal, setting clear expectations, developing a contract, maintaining regular communication, and managing expectations. By following these steps, you can secure an engagement that is beneficial for both parties and sets the foundation for a successful long-term relationship with the client.

Chapter 5
Consulting Best Practices

Consulting best practices are essential to provide high-quality services to clients and maintain the consultant's reputation. It involves following a set of guidelines and methods to ensure that consultants deliver value to their clients. In this chapter, we will discuss some of the best practices in business consulting.

1. Understanding the Client's Needs

The first step in providing consulting services is to understand the client's needs. Consultants should listen to their clients and identify their problems and requirements. They must also analyze the client's business environment, operations, and goals to offer tailored solutions. The consultant's approach should be client-centric, and they should aim to develop a long-term relationship with the client.

2. Setting Clear Goals and Objectives

Once the consultant understands the client's needs, they should define clear goals and objectives. These goals should be specific, measurable, achievable, relevant, and time-bound (SMART). Setting SMART goals allows consultants to track their progress and measure their success. Consultants should also communicate these goals to their clients to ensure that both parties are aligned.

3. Collaborating with the Client

Consultants should collaborate with their clients to achieve their goals. They should work together to identify and prioritize solutions that will add value to the client's business. Collaborating with the client also helps build trust and fosters a sense of ownership in the decision-making process.

4. Conducting a Thorough Analysis

A thorough analysis is essential to identify problems, risks, and opportunities. Consultants should use various tools and methodologies to conduct an analysis of the client's business. They should use data-driven insights and best practices to

© The Author(s), under exclusive license to Springer Nature Switzerland AG 2023
F. Addimando, *Client-Centered Business Consulting*, SpringerBriefs in
Psychology, https://doi.org/10.1007/978-3-031-42844-9_5

develop solutions that are relevant and effective. A thorough analysis helps consultants to provide a comprehensive view of the client's business and enables them to make informed decisions.

5. **Developing a Roadmap**

After conducting a thorough analysis, consultants should develop a roadmap that outlines the steps required to achieve the client's goals. This roadmap should be detailed and include timelines, budgets, and expected outcomes. The roadmap should be reviewed and updated regularly to ensure that it remains relevant to the client's business.

6. **Managing the Project**

Consultants should manage the project efficiently to ensure that it stays on track and within budget. They should set clear expectations with the client and ensure that they communicate regularly to keep them informed of progress. Consultants should also establish a governance framework to manage risks, resolve issues, and make decisions.

7. **Continuous Improvement**

Consultants should continuously improve their services to provide value to their clients. They should measure their performance against their goals and objectives and use feedback to improve their services. Consultants should also stay up-to-date with industry trends, best practices, and emerging technologies to offer innovative solutions to their clients.

8. **Maintaining Professional Standards**

Consultants should maintain professional standards to ensure that they provide high-quality services to their clients. They should adhere to ethical and legal standards and maintain confidentiality at all times. Consultants should also invest in their professional development and training to enhance their skills and knowledge.

In conclusion, following consulting best practices is essential to providing high-quality services to clients and maintaining the consultant's reputation. It involves understanding the client's needs, setting clear goals and objectives, collaborating with the client, conducting a thorough analysis, developing a roadmap, managing the project, continuous improvement, and maintaining professional standards. By following these best practices, consultants can provide value to their clients and achieve long-term success in their careers.

5.1 Defining the Problem

As a business consultant, it is essential to have a clear understanding of the problem that needs to be addressed. Defining the problem is the first step in any consulting engagement, and it sets the foundation for the entire project. In this section, we will explore the process of defining the problem and why it is crucial for successful consulting engagements.

Defining the problem involves identifying the issue or challenge that the client is facing. It requires a deep understanding of the client's business, industry, and context. The problem definition process involves gathering information, analyzing data, and clarifying objectives.

The following are some steps involved in defining the problem:

- Gather information: The first step in defining the problem is to gather information about the client's business. This information can be obtained through interviews with key stakeholders, surveys, or by reviewing the company's financial statements and other relevant documents.
- Analyze data: Once the information has been gathered, it is time to analyze the data. This involves looking for patterns, trends, and insights that can help identify the root cause of the problem. The analysis may involve using statistical techniques, such as regression analysis or hypothesis testing.
- Clarify objectives: After analysing the data, it is essential to clarify the objectives of the engagement. This involves identifying the client's goals and the outcomes they want to achieve through the consulting engagement. It is also essential to identify any constraints or limitations that may impact the engagement.
- Develop a problem statement: Once the objectives have been clarified, it is time to develop a problem statement. This statement should clearly define the problem that the client is facing and the outcomes they want to achieve. The problem statement should be concise and focused to ensure that the consulting engagement remains on track.

Defining the problem is critical to the success of any consulting engagement. It ensures that the consultant and the client have a shared understanding of the issue at hand and the objectives of the engagement. A well-defined problem statement also helps to identify the scope of the engagement and the resources needed to complete the project.

There are several benefits to defining the problem in a consulting engagement. These include:

- Focus: Defining the problem helps to focus the engagement on the issue at hand. It ensures that the consultant and the client are aligned on the objectives of the engagement and the outcomes they want to achieve.
- Efficiency: A well-defined problem statement helps to identify the scope of the engagement and the resources needed to complete the project. This ensures that the engagement is efficient and completed within the agreed-upon time frame.
- Clarity: A clear problem statement helps to ensure that the client and the consultant have a shared understanding of the issue at hand. This clarity can help to avoid misunderstandings and ensure that the engagement remains on track.
- Value: A well-defined problem statement helps to ensure that the consulting engagement delivers value to the client. It ensures that the engagement is focused on addressing the issue at hand and achieving the outcomes that the client desires.

In conclusion, defining the problem is a critical first step in any consulting engagement. It involves gathering information, analyzing data, and clarifying objectives to develop a concise and focused problem statement. A well-defined problem statement helps to ensure that the engagement is efficient, focused, and delivers value to the client. As a business consultant, it is essential to master the process of defining the problem to ensure the success of your consulting engagements.

5.2   Developing a Project Plan

Business consulting is a field that requires strategic planning and efficient execution of ideas to help businesses achieve their goals. One of the crucial aspects of business consulting is developing a project plan that outlines the steps necessary to achieve the desired outcomes. A project plan serves as a guide for both the consultant and the client to ensure that the project runs smoothly and stays on track.

The development of a project plan is a critical stage of the consulting process, and it is important to pay close attention to the details. A well-crafted project plan includes a clear definition of the project, a detailed timeline, and a budget. It also outlines the objectives, deliverables, and scope of the project, as well as the roles and responsibilities of all involved parties.

To start the project planning process, the consultant should first define the problem or opportunity that the project aims to address. This means conducting research and analysis to identify the root cause of the problem or the potential benefits of the opportunity. This information should be gathered through interviews, surveys, data analysis, and any other relevant sources.

Once the problem or opportunity has been clearly defined, the consultant can start developing the project plan. The project plan should include a comprehensive timeline that outlines the specific tasks that need to be completed, along with the deadlines for each task. This timeline should also account for any potential roadblocks or delays that may arise during the project.

In addition to the timeline, the project plan should also include a budget that outlines the costs associated with each task. This budget should be realistic and take into account any potential unforeseen expenses that may arise during the project. The consultant should work closely with the client to ensure that the budget aligns with their financial capabilities and expectations.

Another key element of a project plan is the objectives and deliverables. Objectives should be specific, measurable, achievable, relevant, and time-bound (SMART). The consultant and the client should agree on the objectives and ensure that they align with the overall business strategy. Deliverables should be clearly defined and should outline the specific outputs that will be produced as a result of the project.

The project plan should also clearly define the scope of the project. This means outlining what is included and what is not included in the project. It is important to manage client expectations by ensuring that they understand what the project will achieve and what it will not achieve.

Finally, the project plan should define the roles and responsibilities of all involved parties. This includes the consultant, the client, and any other stakeholders who may be involved in the project. The roles and responsibilities should be clearly defined to ensure that everyone understands their role in the project and what is expected of them.

Overall, developing a project plan is a critical part of the consulting process. It ensures that both the consultant and the client are on the same page and that the project is executed efficiently and effectively. By defining the problem, developing a timeline and budget, outlining the objectives and deliverables, defining the scope of the project, and defining the roles and responsibilities, the consultant can create a roadmap for success.

5.3   Conducting Research and Analysis

Conducting research and analysis is a crucial part of the consulting process. Before developing any recommendations or solutions for a client, a consultant must first gather data and information about the client's business and industry. This information can come from a variety of sources, including interviews with key stakeholders, industry reports, financial statements, and market research.

One of the first steps in conducting research and analysis is to identify the key issues or challenges facing the client. This can be done through a combination of interviews with the client's management team, a review of the company's financial performance, and an analysis of the competitive landscape in the industry.

Once the key issues have been identified, the consultant can begin gathering data to support their analysis. This may involve conducting surveys of customers or employees, reviewing market research reports, or analysing financial statements to understand the client's revenue streams and cost structures.

Another important aspect of conducting research and analysis is to understand the client's industry and competitors. This can involve reviewing industry reports and publications, attending industry conferences and events, and conducting benchmarking studies to understand how the client's performance compares to others in the industry.

The consultant may also need to conduct a SWOT analysis to identify the client's strengths, weaknesses, opportunities, and threats. This can be done through interviews with key stakeholders, a review of financial statements, and an analysis of industry trends and market data.

Once the data has been gathered, the consultant can begin to analyze it to identify trends and patterns. This may involve using statistical software to analyze large data sets or conducting qualitative analysis to identify themes and insights.

Once the analysis is complete, the consultant can begin to develop recommendations and solutions for the client. These recommendations should be based on a deep understanding of the client's business and industry, as well as a thorough analysis of the data.

Throughout the research and analysis process, it's important for the consultant to communicate regularly with the client to ensure that they are on track and that their recommendations are aligned with the client's goals. This may involve presenting findings and insights to the client's management team or holding regular check-in meetings to discuss progress and next steps.

In summary, conducting research and analysis is a critical step in the consulting process. It allows consultants to gain a deep understanding of their client's business and industry, identify key issues and challenges, and develop recommendations and solutions based on data and insights. By following a rigorous and thorough research and analysis process, consultants can provide value to their clients and help them achieve their goals.

5.4   Creating Actionable Recommendations

As a business consultant, your ultimate goal is to provide your client with actionable recommendations that can help improve their operations, increase efficiency, and ultimately drive revenue growth. The process of creating these recommendations is complex and multifaceted and requires careful planning, analysis, and communication.

In this section, we'll discuss the key steps involved in creating actionable recommendations as part of a consulting engagement. These steps include identifying key issues, conducting research and analysis, brainstorming potential solutions, evaluating alternatives, and presenting your recommendations in a clear and compelling way.

5.4.1   Step 1: Identifying Key Issues

The first step in creating actionable recommendations is to identify the key issues that are impacting your client's business. This may involve conducting interviews with key stakeholders, reviewing financial statements and other data, and conducting a SWOT analysis to identify strengths, weaknesses, opportunities, and threats.

As you work to identify key issues, it's important to keep in mind that not all problems are created equal. Some issues may be symptoms of a larger problem, while others may be critical issues that require immediate attention. By identifying the most important issues upfront, you can focus your research and analysis efforts on those areas that are most likely to have the greatest impact.

5.4.2 Step 2: Conducting Research and Analysis

Once you've identified key issues, the next step is to conduct research and analysis to better understand the root causes of these issues. This may involve reviewing industry reports and benchmarking data, conducting market research, and analyzing financial data to identify trends and patterns.

It's important to approach this research and analysis phase with an open mind and to be willing to challenge your assumptions and preconceptions. By gathering data and insights from a variety of sources, you can develop a more comprehensive understanding of the challenges your client is facing and identify potential solutions that may not have been immediately apparent.

5.4.3 Step 3: Brainstorming Potential Solutions

Once you've conducted your research and analysis, the next step is to brainstorm potential solutions to address the key issues you've identified. This may involve working with your client's team to develop new processes, procedures, or systems or identifying opportunities to streamline existing operations.

As you work through this process, it's important to keep in mind that not all solutions are created equal. Some solutions may be more feasible or cost-effective than others, while others may require significant investment or resources. By considering a range of potential solutions, you can identify those that are most likely to drive the greatest impact and return on investment.

5.4.4 Step 4: Evaluating Alternatives

Once you've brainstormed potential solutions, the next step is to evaluate these alternatives to identify the best course of action. This may involve conducting a cost-benefit analysis to identify the potential ROI of different options or a risk assessment to identify potential risks and uncertainties.

As you evaluate potential alternatives, it's important to consider a range of factors, including the feasibility of each option, the level of investment required, and the potential impact on your client's operations. By taking a comprehensive, data-driven approach to evaluating alternatives, you can identify the best course of action to address the key issues facing your client.

5.4.5 Step 5: Presenting Recommendations

The final step in creating actionable recommendations is to present your findings and recommendations to your client in a clear and compelling way. This may involve creating a detailed report outlining your analysis and recommendations or presenting your findings in a more visual format, such as a PowerPoint presentation.

As you prepare your recommendations, it's important to keep in mind the needs and preferences of your audience. Some clients may prefer a more data-driven approach, while others may respond better to a more narrative presentation style. By tailoring your presentation to the needs and preferences of your client, you can increase the likelihood that your recommendations will be accepted and implemented.

5.5 Delivering Effective Presentations

Delivering effective presentations is a critical aspect of business consulting. As a consultant, you will need to convey complex ideas and recommendations to clients, often to stakeholders who may not have the same level of expertise or understanding as you. Presentations provide an opportunity to showcase your expertise, build credibility, and persuade stakeholders to take action.

To deliver an effective presentation, you need to do more than simply create slides and speak clearly. A successful presentation requires careful planning, preparation, and execution. Here are some key elements to consider:

1. Audience analysis: Before you start creating your presentation, you need to consider who your audience is and what their needs and expectations are. Are they technical experts, or are they nonexperts? What are their goals and objectives? What is their level of knowledge about the subject matter? Answering these questions will help you tailor your presentation to your audience's specific needs.
2. Content development: Once you understand your audience, you can start developing your content. Your content should be organized, relevant, and easy to understand. You should use clear, concise language and avoid technical jargon. Visual aids such as graphs, charts, and images can help illustrate your points and make your presentation more engaging.
3. Delivery techniques: When it comes to delivering your presentation, there are several techniques you can use to make your message more impactful. These include using storytelling to create an emotional connection with your audience, humor to break the ice and keep the audience engaged, and repetition to reinforce key points.
4. Visual design: The visual design of your presentation is also critical. Your slides should be visually appealing, easy to read, and uncluttered. You should use a consistent design throughout your presentation, including colours, fonts, and graphics.

5. Rehearsal: Finally, it's important to rehearse your presentation before you deliver it. This will help you feel more confident and prepared, and will also help you identify any issues with your content or delivery. You should practice delivering your presentation several times and consider recording yourself so that you can review and refine your delivery.

In addition to these key elements, there are several best practices that can help ensure your presentation is effective. These include:

- Start with a strong opening: Your opening should grab the audience's attention and set the tone for the rest of the presentation. Consider starting with a provocative question or an interesting anecdote.
- Use clear transitions: Your transitions should help guide the audience through your presentation and keep them engaged. Make sure your transitions are clear and easy to follow.
- Limit your content: Don't overload your audience with too much information. Instead, focus on the most important points and keep your presentation concise.
- Practice active listening: During the Q&A portion of your presentation, make sure to actively listen to your audience's questions and concerns. This will help you build rapport and establish credibility.
- Follow up: After your presentation, be sure to follow up with your audience to address any additional questions or concerns they may have.

Overall, delivering effective presentations is a critical skill for business consultants. By understanding your audience, developing compelling content, and delivering your message in a clear and engaging way, you can build credibility and persuade stakeholders to take action.

Chapter 6
How to Set the Right Price

6.1 Cost Analysis

The first point to consider when setting the right price for business consultancy is the cost analysis. This step is essential to ensure that the price offered covers all costs associated with providing the service, enabling the professional to carry out their work effectively without having to suffer financial losses.

To carry out an accurate cost analysis, the consultant must consider several factors. The first is the time spent consulting. It is important to calculate the time spent on the various phases of the project, such as planning, preparation, implementation and evaluation of results. This will allow you to evaluate the hourly cost of the work and to charge the correct amount for the time dedicated to consulting.

Secondly, the professional must consider travel expenses. If the project requires the presence of the consultant at the client company, it will be necessary to include travel expenses, such as the cost of airfare or fuel, accommodation, and meals. Even if not all activities require the physical presence of the professional at the client company, it is still important to take these expenses into consideration, so as not to underestimate the costs associated with the consultancy.

In addition, the professional must consider any fees to be paid to other professionals involved in the project. For example, if the consultant must work with an attorney or accountant to complete the project, the fees paid to these professionals should be included in the overall costs of the consultancy. Finally, the trader must take into consideration their desired profit margin. This may vary depending on the professional's level of experience and reputation, but must be adequate to cover the costs of the business and generate sufficient profit.

Cost analysis can be a complex task and requires time and attention to detail. However, it is essential to ensure that the price being offered is fair and that the professional can provide the best possible service without incurring financial loss.

F. Addimando, *Client-Centered Business Consulting*, SpringerBriefs in Psychology, https://doi.org/10.1007/978-3-031-42844-9_6

In conclusion, cost analysis is the first important step to consider when setting the right price for a business consultancy.

By taking into consideration the time spent consulting, travel expenses, commissions of the professionals involved, and the desired profit margin, the professional can ensure that the price offered covers all costs associated with the consultation and generates an adequate profit. While it takes time and attention to detail, cost analysis is essential to ensure that the professional delivers the best possible service to their clients.

6.2   Evaluation of the Demand

The second point to consider when setting the right price for business consultancy is the value of the service offered. The value of the service refers to the benefit that the client obtains from the consultancy and can be used as a criterion for determining the price. To evaluate the value of the service, the professional must consider several factors. The first is the level of expertise and experience of the practitioner.

If the professional has extensive industry experience and a positive reputation, the value of the service can be increased. Second, the professional must consider the added value that the consultancy can provide to the client company. For example, if the consultancy can help the company improve its production processes or reduce costs, the value of the service will be greater.

Additionally, the practitioner must consider the value that counseling can provide over the long term. If the consultancy can help the client company achieve long-term goals, such as increasing sales or reducing operating costs, the value of the service will be greater than with a short-term consultancy.

Finally, the professional must consider the financial situation of the client company. If the company is in a difficult financial situation, it may be necessary to offer a lower price for consultancy to maintain the economic viability of the project. However, if the company has an adequate budget and seeks high quality advice, the price offered may be higher. In conclusion, the value of the service is an important criterion to consider when setting the right price for a business consultancy.

Taking into consideration the level of expertise of the professional, the added value that the consultancy can provide to the client company, the long-term value and the financial situation of the client company, the professional can determine a price that reflects the value of the service offered. Offering an appropriate price can help ensure customer satisfaction and repeat business in the future.

6.3   Benchmarking

The third point to consider when setting the right price for business consultancy is competition. It is important for the trader to consider the prices offered by competitors, but it should not be the sole determining factor in choosing the price.

The professional must consider the added value it offers compared to the competition. If the professional offers a high quality service, with extensive industry experience and demonstrable results, the price offered may be higher than the competition.

Furthermore, the trader must consider the position of the market in which he is located. While most professionals in the local market offer lower prices, the professional must consider price reduction to be competitive. Conversely, if the professional offers a high level of service and stands out from the competition, the price could be increased to reflect the added value.

The trader also needs to consider price positioning relative to the competition. Offering prices that are too low can make the service seem low-quality and uncompetitive with the competition. On the other hand, offering prices that are too high can be uncompetitive and drive away customers.

The professional should try to find a price that is in the mid-range, which is competitive but which reflects the value of the service being offered. Finally, the trader should also consider the global market, not just the local one. If the trader offers a service that can be used worldwide, he must consider the price offered by competitors globally.

If the price offered is too high compared to global competition, it may be difficult to attract customers. In conclusion, competition is an important factor to consider when setting the right price for business consultancy. However, it shouldn't be the only determining factor in choosing the price.

The trader should consider the added value it offers compared to the competition, the position of the market in which it is located and the positioning of the prices compared to the competition. Setting an appropriate and competitive price can help ensure customer satisfaction and repeat business in the future.

6.4   Offer of Customized Packages

The fourth point to consider when setting the right price for a business consultancy is the type of customer you are trying to reach. Different types of clients may have different needs and budgets, and the professional must adjust the price according to these differences. For example, if the professional is trying to reach small businesses or startups, they may need to offer a lower price to be competitive.

Small businesses may not have the ability to pay high prices, but they could still benefit from business consulting. The professional might also consider offering affordable service packages for startups that have limited budgets. On the other hand, if the professional is trying to reach large companies, it may be necessary to offer a higher price to reflect the complexity of the work and the quality of service required.

Large companies may have more financial resources at their disposal and may be willing to pay a higher price for top-notch business advice. The practitioner should also consider the type of industry in which the client operates. Some industries, such as finance or medical, require specialized advice and may be willing to pay a higher price for such a service. Conversely, other industries may require less specialization and the price may be lower. Furthermore, the practitioner should also consider the geographic location of the client.

Living costs and income levels may vary based on the region or country where the customer is located. For example, living costs in big cities can be higher than in rural areas, and the price could be adjusted accordingly. Finally, the practitioner should also consider whether the client is a repeat client or a new client. Regular customers may be willing to pay a higher price if they have had positive experiences with the professional in the past.

On the other hand, new customers may request a lower price to test the service before committing more significantly. In conclusion, the type of client you are trying to reach is an important factor to consider when setting the right price for business consultancy.

The practitioner should adjust the price based on the client's needs and budget, the type of industry the client operates in, the client's geographic location, and whether the client is a repeat client or a new client. Setting an appropriate and customized price based on the customer's needs can help ensure customer satisfaction and repeat business in the future.

6.5 Evaluation of the Added Value

The evaluation of the added value is an important tool for analysing and measuring the success of a business consultancy. The added value represents the difference between the total value generated by the consultancy project and the costs incurred to implement the project itself. In other words, the added value represents the contribution that the consultancy has provided to the client and to his business.

The evaluation of the added value is an important process for the business consultancy professional because it allows to quantify the contribution of the consultancy to the client company. This is especially helpful because counseling outcomes can be difficult to objectively measure and quantify. Evaluating added value can be done using a variety of methods, including ROI (return on investment) analysis or NPV (net present value) analysis. ROI analysis calculates the relationship between the value generated by the project and the costs incurred to implement the project, while NPV analysis calculates the present value of future cash flows generated by the project.

In both cases, the consulting professional must be able to quantify the value generated by the consulting project and compare it with the costs incurred to implement the project. In this way, the professional can demonstrate to the client the value of the advice provided and justify the price charged for the work performed. The evaluation of the added value can also be useful for the customer himself. Indeed, the client can use the evaluation results to justify the cost of the consultancy within the company and demonstrate the added value of the consultancy for the company itself.

However, it is important to remember that assessing the added value should not be the only criterion for evaluating the success of a consultancy project. Consulting can have an added value that is not immediately quantifiable, such as the acquisition of new skills and knowledge by the client, the creation of relationships of trust and collaboration, or the improvement of organizational culture.

Value added assessment is an important tool for quantifying the contribution of business consultancy and justifying the price charged for the work performed. However, it is also important to consider other factors, such as improved client relationships and skills, to evaluate the success of a consulting project.

6.6   Risk Management

Risk management is a crucial aspect of business consulting, as businesses are constantly faced with situations that present uncertainty and risk. Risk management consists of identifying, assessing and mitigating the risks associated with a specific activity. Risk management not only helps prevent the loss of assets, but also minimizes the impact of any unforeseen events. Typically, risk management is implemented through a five-step process: risk identification, risk assessment, risk mitigation, risk monitoring, and ongoing assessment.

In the identification phase, the potential risks associated with the specific activity are identified. In the evaluation phase, the degree to which an event is likely to occur and the impact it would have on the business is assessed. In the mitigation phase, steps are taken to reduce the likelihood of an event occurring or the impact it would have on the business. In the monitoring phase, the risks are continuously monitored to ensure that the mitigation measures are effective.

Finally, in the continuous assessment phase, it is assessed whether the risk management process has been effective and whether further measures are needed to mitigate the risks. Risk management is critical in every area of business, but is especially important in high-risk industries such as finance, power generation, chemicals, healthcare, and transportation. In these areas, risk management is essential not only for the survival of the company but also for the safety of the public and the preservation of the environment. Business consulting can play an important role in risk management.

Consulting professionals can help businesses identify the specific risks associated with their operations, assess the level of risk, and develop effective strategies to mitigate the risks. Additionally, consulting can help businesses understand the regulations and laws that affect risk management, ensuring that the business is compliant with legal and regulatory requirements.

Risk management is also important for small businesses. Even though small businesses may have fewer risks to manage than large companies, they can still be exposed to significant risk. For example, a small business that depends on a single supplier for a raw material could be seriously hurt if the supplier experiences a price hike or goes bankrupt. Risk management helps small businesses identify risks and develop strategies to manage them, ensuring their long-term survival.

6.7 Pricing Strategies

Pricing strategies are critical to the success of any business, including business consulting. It is a complex and delicate process which requires a thorough understanding of the target market, the competition the customers and the costs incurred by the company. In this section, we will look at the different pricing strategies that can be used by consulting firms to set the price of their services. The first pricing strategy we will look at is cost-plus-margin pricing.

This technique involves adding a fixed margin to the cost of services, in order to guarantee a profit for the company. This strategy is relatively simple to implement, but can pose some challenges in terms of competitiveness. Indeed, if the price is too high compared to the competition, clients may choose other consulting firms.

The second pricing strategy is that of competition-based pricing. In this case, the consulting firm takes into consideration the price of the services offered by its competitors, and tries to adjust its price in order to be competitive on the market. This strategy can be effective if competitors offer similar services and the market is fairly homogeneous, but it can lead to a loss in perceived value if the consulting firm simply competes on price.

The third pricing strategy we will look at is value-based pricing. This technique involves fixing the price of services based on the value perceived by customers, or the benefit that the services offer them. In practice, the consulting firm should try to understand the specific needs of its clients and propose customized solutions that respond to those needs. This strategy can be very effective in differentiating the consulting firm from the competition and enhancing the services offered.

The fourth pricing strategy that we will examine is that of differentiated pricing. In this case, the consulting firm sets different prices for different services, based on the specificity of the clients' needs, their financial situation, the sector in which they operate, and so on.

This strategy can be effective if the consulting firm can identify the most profitable market segments and offer customized solutions for each one. Finally, we'll look at the dynamic pricing strategy, which involves varying the price of services based on market conditions. For example, if the demand for consulting services is high, the firm might raise the price to make the most of the market situation.

Conversely, if demand is low, the company may lower its price to incentivize customers to use its services. This pricing strategy is based on the idea that customers are willing to pay more for a product or service that is unique or offers added value compared to the competition. In this way, the company can justify a higher price due to the perception of high quality and value offered to the customer.

Another approach to pricing strategy is dynamic pricing. This strategy consists of adjusting the price according to fluctuations in supply and demand. For example, in a period of high demand, the company might raise the price of its product or service, while in a period of low demand, it might lower it to stimulate sales.

This strategy requires good market knowledge and a constant demand monitoring system. Another common strategy is that of penetration pricing. This approach involves setting an initial low price to penetrate the market and gain market share. Once the business has gained a loyal customer base, it can gradually raise the price of the product or service to make more profit. This strategy is particularly effective when the company has an innovative and unique product or service on the market.

Finally, the company might adopt a bundle pricing strategy, which involves selling several products or services as a package at a lower price than buying each individual product or service separately. This strategy is effective when the business has several products or services that are related to each other so that customers can benefit from purchasing multiple products or services as a bundle.

Ultimately, choosing the right pricing strategy depends on the specific needs of the company, the product or service offered, the reference market, and the competition. A well-planned and properly implemented pricing strategy can help your business maximize profits, gain market share, and keep customers satisfied.

6.8 Price Communication

Price communication is an essential component of a company's pricing strategy. Effective price communication can influence customers' perception of the value of your product or service and improve your company's reputation. On the other hand, miscommunication of price can lead to misunderstandings and a negative perception of the value offered by the company. One of the key aspects of price communication is transparency.

The company must provide clear and detailed information about the price of the product or service, including any incidental costs, such as shipping costs, taxes, and other fees. This can help build customer trust in the company and improve their perception of the value provided. In addition, the company must consider the right time to communicate the price. For example, if the price of the product or service is too high compared to the competition, it can be useful to communicate in advance the benefits and the added value that the product or service offers. Conversely, if the price is lower than the competition, the company may use price communication to emphasize the opportunity for savings. Another important aspect is the choice of communication channels. The company must choose the most effective communication channels to reach its customers.

For example, effective price communication might include advertising on social media, sending personalized emails to customers, or posting ads on price comparison websites. Furthermore, the company must consider the language used in the communication of the price. The language must be clear and easily understandable for customers, avoiding jargon and complex sentences. Using simple, direct language can help improve understanding of the value of your product or service and make it easier for customers to make decisions.

Finally, the company must pay attention to consistency in the communication of the price. This means that the price communicated must be consistent across all channels used by the company and with the actual price of the product or service. Lack of consistency in price communication can lead to confusion and distrust among customers. In summary, price communication is a key element in a company's pricing strategy.

Effective price communication can influence customers' perception of the value of your product or service and improve your company's reputation. To achieve the best results, the company should adopt a transparent approach, choose the most effective communication channels, use simple and direct language, and maintain consistency in price communication.

Chapter 7
Practical Advice for Effective Consultation

Effective consultation is the key to the success of any consulting project. However, being an effective consultant involves more than just technical knowledge and skills. It also involves effective communication, relationship-building, and problem-solving skills. In this chapter, we will discuss some practical advice for effective consultation that can help you achieve your consulting goals.

One of the most important skills that a consultant can possess is active listening. Active listening involves fully engaging with the client and paying close attention to their concerns, needs, and objectives. It means asking open-ended questions, seeking clarification when necessary, and taking the time to truly understand the client's perspective.

Active listening is critical for building rapport with the client, establishing trust, and demonstrating empathy. It also helps you identify the underlying issues and challenges that the client is facing, which can help you develop more effective solutions.

Effective communication is essential for successful consulting. It involves not only clearly conveying your ideas and recommendations but also actively engaging with the client and seeking feedback.

To communicate effectively, you need to use language that is clear, concise, and easy to understand. You also need to be aware of nonverbal cues such as tone of voice and body language, which can convey a great deal of information.

It's important to keep the client informed throughout the project, providing regular updates on progress and soliciting feedback at every stage. This helps build trust and confidence in your abilities as a consultant.

Consulting projects can be complex and unpredictable, and you need to be able to adapt to changing circumstances and evolving client needs. This requires a high degree of flexibility and adaptability.

Being flexible means being open to new ideas and approaches and being willing to modify your plans as needed. It also means being able to work effectively under pressure and in challenging circumstances.

F. Addimando, *Client-Centered Business Consulting*, SpringerBriefs in
Psychology, https://doi.org/10.1007/978-3-031-42844-9_7

Adaptability means being able to tailor your approach to the specific needs and requirements of each client. This requires a deep understanding of the client's business, as well as the ability to quickly learn new skills and adapt to new technologies and methodologies.

Effective consulting requires a problem-solving mindset. This involves being able to identify the root causes of problems, generate creative solutions, and implement those solutions in a timely and effective manner.

To develop a problem-solving mindset, you need to be able to think critically and analytically, and to approach problems in a structured and systematic way. You also need to be able to generate multiple solutions and evaluate them based on their feasibility and impact.

Building strong relationships with clients is essential for effective consulting. This involves not only establishing trust and rapport but also actively seeking to understand the client's needs, objectives, and concerns.

To build strong relationships, you need to be able to communicate effectively, demonstrate empathy, and establish a clear understanding of the client's expectations. You also need to be responsive to the client's needs, providing regular updates and soliciting feedback throughout the project.

The world of business and consulting is constantly evolving, and you need to stay up-to-date with the latest trends, technologies, and methodologies. This requires a commitment to ongoing learning and professional development.

To stay up-to-date, you need to be curious and open to new ideas, and willing to invest time and effort in staying informed. You also need to be proactive in seeking out new learning opportunities, such as training programs, conferences, and workshops.

Innovation is essential for effective consulting. This involves not only applying the latest technologies and methodologies but also being willing to take risks and try new approaches.

7.1 Setting the Right Price

Setting the right price is a crucial aspect of business consulting, as it can greatly impact both the consultant's bottom line and the client's perception of the value of the services provided. There are several factors to consider when setting a price for consulting services, including the consultant's level of expertise, the complexity of the project, the client's budget, and the competition in the market.

One common approach to pricing consulting services is to charge an hourly rate. This can work well for smaller projects or for clients who are unsure of the scope of work required. However, hourly rates can be difficult to estimate accurately, and clients may be hesitant to agree to an open-ended arrangement.

Another approach is to set a fixed fee for the project. This can provide clients with greater clarity and predictability in terms of costs and can also motivate consultants to work more efficiently to complete the project within the agreed-upon time frame. However, fixed fees can be difficult to calculate accurately, as unforeseen complications or changes in scope can arise during the project.

A third approach is value-based pricing, which involves setting a price based on the value that the consulting services will provide to the client. This can be particularly effective for complex projects that require a high level of expertise, as it allows consultants to charge a premium for their unique skill set and experience. However, value-based pricing can be challenging to implement, as it requires a deep understanding of the client's needs and goals, as well as the potential impact of the consulting services on the client's business.

Regardless of the pricing model chosen, it is important for consultants to communicate clearly with clients about their fees and the scope of work included. This can help to build trust and ensure that both parties have a clear understanding of the expectations for the project.

When determining the appropriate price for consulting services, it is also important to consider the costs associated with running a consulting business. This includes not only the consultant's time and expertise but also expenses such as marketing, office space, and travel. It can be helpful to track these costs closely and to adjust pricing accordingly to ensure that the business remains profitable.

Finally, it is important to remain flexible when setting prices for consulting services. As the market and client needs evolve, consultants may need to adjust their pricing strategies in order to remain competitive and to continue providing value to their clients. By staying attuned to market trends and client feedback, consultants can ensure that they are setting the right price for their services, while also maintaining a profitable and sustainable business model.

7.2   What to Bring

In the world of business consulting, being prepared for any situation is key. This includes having the necessary tools and materials on hand to make a successful and impactful presentation. In this chapter, we will discuss what items to bring with you when meeting with clients, as well as how to ensure you are fully prepared for the meeting.

The first step in preparing for a meeting is to gather all relevant materials. This includes any reports, charts, or graphs that you may need to present to the client. It is important to ensure that these materials are not only up-to-date but also relevant to the client's needs. This may require some additional research to fully understand the client's business and their specific challenges.

Another important consideration is the technology you will need to present your materials. This could include a laptop or tablet, as well as any necessary cords or adapters. You should also bring a backup copy of your presentation on a USB drive or in the cloud, in case there are any technical issues with your primary device.

In addition to the materials and technology, it is also important to bring any necessary paperwork or contracts. This may include an agreement outlining the terms of your services or a nondisclosure agreement to protect the client's confidential information. You should also bring a pen and paper to take notes during the meeting.

In some cases, it may also be appropriate to bring samples of your work or previous client success stories. This can help to illustrate your experience and expertise and give the client a better understanding of what you can offer.

When deciding what to bring to a meeting, it is important to consider the specific needs and preferences of the client. For example, if the client has requested a specific type of presentation or format, it is important to adhere to those guidelines. You may also want to consider the client's company culture and dress code when selecting your attire for the meeting.

Beyond physical materials, it is also important to prepare mentally for the meeting. This includes doing research on the client and their industry, as well as practising your presentation beforehand. It is also important to have a clear understanding of your goals and objectives for the meeting, as well as any potential challenges or objections that may arise.

In addition to being prepared, it is also important to be flexible and adaptable during the meeting. This includes being able to adjust your presentation or approach based on the client's feedback or changing needs. It is also important to actively listen to the client's concerns and feedback and be willing to make adjustments to your recommendations based on their input.

In conclusion, preparing for a client meeting requires careful consideration of both physical materials and mental preparation. By gathering all necessary materials, doing your research, and having a clear understanding of your objectives, you can set yourself up for a successful meeting. Additionally, being flexible and adaptable during the meeting can help to build trust and rapport with the client and ultimately lead to a successful consulting engagement.

7.3 Dressing for Success

In the world of business consulting, making the right impression is essential. The way you present yourself can have a significant impact on the way clients perceive you and your abilities. This is why dressing for success is an important aspect of business consulting that cannot be overlooked. In this section, we will discuss the importance of dressing for success and provide some practical tips for consultants to consider.

The first reason why dressing for success is important is that it helps to establish credibility. When you dress professionally, clients are more likely to view you as an expert in your field. It shows that you take your work seriously and are committed to delivering high-quality results. Additionally, dressing appropriately for the occasion helps to create a positive first impression, which is essential in building a strong client relationship.

Another reason why dressing for success is important is that it helps to build trust. When you dress professionally, clients are more likely to trust you with their business. They feel more confident in your abilities and are more likely to take your recommendations seriously. This trust can be critical in securing future business from clients and building a reputation as a reliable and trustworthy consultant.

Dressing for success also helps to create a sense of professionalism. When you dress appropriately, it sends a message to clients that you take your work seriously and are dedicated to providing the best possible service. This can be particularly important in industries where professionalism is highly valued, such as finance, law, or healthcare.

So, what does dressing for success actually look like? While the specific attire can vary depending on the industry and occasion, there are some general guidelines that all consultants should follow. Here are some practical tips to consider:

- Dress for the occasion: It's important to dress appropriately for the specific occasion. If you're meeting with a client at their office, for example, you may need to dress more formally than if you're meeting at a casual coffee shop. Consider the context of the meeting and dress accordingly.
- Keep it simple: Avoid flashy or distracting clothing and accessories. Stick to neutral colors and classic styles that are appropriate for the occasion.
- Pay attention to details: Make sure your clothing is clean, pressed, and well-maintained. Pay attention to details like your shoes, belt, and accessories to ensure that everything is in good condition.
- Avoid strong fragrances: Strong fragrances can be distracting and even offensive to some people. Stick to a light and subtle scent, or avoid wearing fragrance altogether.
- Consider the culture: Different cultures have different expectations when it comes to dress. If you're working with clients from a different culture, take some time to understand their expectations and adjust your attire accordingly.
- Be comfortable: While it's important to dress appropriately, it's also important to be comfortable. If you're uncomfortable in your clothing, it can be distracting and even impact your performance. Choose clothing that is both appropriate and comfortable.

In conclusion, dressing for success is an important aspect of business consulting that should not be overlooked. It helps to establish credibility, build trust, and create a sense of professionalism. By following some simple guidelines and paying attention to the context of the occasion, consultants can ensure that they are presenting themselves in the best possible light to their clients.

7.4 Using Appropriate Language

Language is a powerful tool that consultants use to communicate with clients. The language used can determine how the consultant is perceived by the client and can greatly affect the outcome of the engagement. Business consultants need to be able to communicate effectively using appropriate language in order to build trust, establish credibility, and convey complex information to clients. In this section, we will discuss the importance of using appropriate language in business consulting and provide some tips on how to use language effectively.

Using appropriate language is critical to building a successful relationship with a client. It is important to use language that is clear and concise, and that conveys professionalism and expertise. Using the wrong language can lead to misunderstandings, miscommunication, and a breakdown in trust between the consultant and the client. Furthermore, using inappropriate language can give the impression that the consultant lacks knowledge or experience in their field. Using the appropriate language can help a consultant establish credibility and build trust with their client. Clients want to work with consultants who are knowledgeable and experienced, and who can clearly communicate their ideas and recommendations. Consultants who use appropriate language are viewed as being more professional and trustworthy, which can help them build a strong relationship with their clients.

Here are some tips for using appropriate language in business consulting:

- Use simple and clear language: Business consultants should avoid using jargon, technical terms, or complex language that their clients may not understand. Instead, they should use simple and clear language that conveys their ideas in a way that is easy for clients to understand.
- Be concise: Consultants should avoid using long-winded sentences or paragraphs. Instead, they should use short, concise sentences that get to the point quickly and effectively.
- Know your audience: Different clients have different levels of knowledge and expertise. A consultant should tailor their language to the audience they are speaking to. For example, if the client is a nontechnical person, the consultant should avoid using technical language that may confuse them.
- Avoid negative language: Consultants should avoid using negative language, such as "problem," "failure," or "mistake." Instead, they should use positive language, such as "challenge," "opportunity," or "improvement." This can help to create a more positive and productive atmosphere for the engagement.
- Use active voice: Using active voice can help to make language more clear and concise. For example, instead of saying "the report was written by the team," say "the team wrote the report."
- Avoid using absolutes: Consultants should avoid using absolutes, such as "always," "never," or "completely." These types of words can come across as rigid and inflexible, and can limit the potential solutions for the engagement.
- Use visual aids: Consultants can use visual aids, such as graphs or charts, to help convey complex information in a way that is easy for clients to understand. This can be especially helpful when dealing with technical or complex issues.

Using appropriate language is critical to building a successful relationship with a client in business consulting. Consultants should use language that is clear, concise, and professional and that conveys their expertise and credibility. By following the tips provided in this article, consultants can effectively use language to communicate with clients and help them achieve their goals.

7.5   Understanding Cultural Differences

As businesses continue to expand globally, it is becoming increasingly important for consultants to understand and navigate cultural differences. Cultural differences can influence the way people think, behave, and communicate in the workplace. In order to provide effective consulting services, consultants need to have a good understanding of the cultural norms and values of their clients.

One of the first steps in understanding cultural differences is to become familiar with the client's country and culture. Consultants should learn about the history, customs, and traditions of the client's country. They should also familiarize themselves with the local business practices and etiquette.

Consultants should be aware of the communication styles that are common in the client's country. For example, in some cultures, people tend to be more indirect in their communication. They may use euphemisms and polite language to convey their message. In other cultures, people tend to be more direct and assertive. Consultants should adapt their communication style to match the client's preferences.

Another important factor to consider when working with clients from different cultures is the concept of "face." In some cultures, saving face and avoiding embarrassment is extremely important. Consultants should be sensitive to this and avoid criticizing the client or making them feel uncomfortable in any way.

Consultants should also be aware of the differences in business practices and customs. For example, in some cultures, it is customary to build a relationship and establish trust before discussing business. In other cultures, business is conducted in a more direct and transactional manner. Consultants should adapt their approach to match the local business culture.

In addition to cultural differences, consultants should also be aware of language barriers. Language differences can cause misunderstandings and hinder effective communication. Consultants should make an effort to learn the local language or work with a translator to ensure that communication is clear and effective.

Finally, consultants should be aware of their own cultural biases and assumptions. Everyone has their own cultural lens through which they view the world. It is important for consultants to recognize their own biases and work to overcome them. This can be achieved by listening to the client and being open to new ideas and perspectives.

Understanding cultural differences is a critical skill for business consultants. Consultants who are able to navigate cultural differences are better equipped to provide effective consulting services to their clients. By becoming familiar with the client's country and culture, adapting their communication style, being aware of business practices and customs, addressing language barriers, and recognizing their own cultural biases, consultants can build strong relationships with clients from different cultures and provide valuable services.

7.6 Managing Client Expectations

Managing client expectations is a critical component of business consulting that ensures a successful engagement. Consulting engagements involve multiple stakeholders, including the consultant, the client, and possibly other third-party vendors, making it vital to have clear communication and a shared understanding of what is expected from all parties involved. If expectations are not properly set and managed, the project can quickly become unproductive, leading to dissatisfaction, wasted time and resources, and potential financial loss.

The following are some practical tips for managing client expectations:

- Be transparent: Transparency is key to managing client expectations. At the beginning of the project, make sure to provide the client with a clear understanding of what to expect from the project, including timelines, deliverables, and budget. Make sure to be transparent about any limitations or challenges that may arise during the project.
- Develop a project plan: A project plan provides a roadmap for the project and outlines the scope, timelines, deliverables, and budget. This document should be agreed upon by both the consultant and the client, and any changes or adjustments should be clearly communicated and agreed upon.
- Provide regular updates: Regular updates help to keep the client informed of the project's progress, any challenges encountered, and any changes made to the project plan. These updates should be provided in a timely manner and should include a summary of accomplishments, a review of any outstanding issues, and any upcoming milestones.
- Set clear communication channels: Establish clear communication channels with the client, including the frequency and type of communication. For example, if weekly status reports are required, make sure to deliver them consistently and on time. This helps to ensure that everyone involved in the project is on the same page and helps to avoid any misunderstandings.
- Manage scope creep: Scope creep refers to the tendency for the scope of the project to expand beyond its original boundaries. Managing scope creep is important to ensure that the project stays within budget and on schedule. If the client requests additional work outside of the original project scope, make sure to communicate the impact on the budget and timeline and obtain approval before proceeding.
- Be responsive: Responsiveness is critical to managing client expectations. Responding to emails and calls in a timely manner shows the client that you are committed to the project and are available to address any concerns or questions they may have.
- Manage conflicts: Conflict can arise during any consulting engagement, and it is important to manage it proactively to avoid derailing the project. Address conflicts in a timely manner, listen to all parties involved, and work collaboratively to find a resolution that is acceptable to everyone.

- Close out the project effectively: At the end of the project, make sure to close out the project effectively. This includes providing the client with all deliverables, obtaining their sign-off on the project, and conducting a final review to ensure that all expectations were met.

Managing client expectations is a critical component of successful consulting engagements. It requires clear communication, transparency, and a shared understanding of what is expected from all parties involved. By following the practical tips outlined above, consultants can effectively manage client expectations and deliver successful projects that meet or exceed their clients' expectations.

7.7 Building Rapport

Building rapport is a key aspect of successful business consulting. It refers to the development of a positive and meaningful relationship between the consultant and the client. When building rapport, the consultant aims to create a sense of trust and understanding that leads to a more productive working relationship. In this section, we will discuss the importance of building rapport in business consulting, and offer tips on how to build rapport with clients.

Why Is Building Rapport Important in Business Consulting?
Building rapport is important in business consulting for several reasons. First, it helps to establish trust between the consultant and the client. Trust is essential in any business relationship, but particularly so in consulting, where the consultant is often brought in to provide an objective perspective on complex business problems. Without trust, the client may be hesitant to share sensitive information or take the consultant's recommendations seriously.

Second, building rapport can help to create a more productive working relationship. When the client and consultant have a good rapport, they are more likely to communicate openly and honestly, share ideas, and work collaboratively toward a common goal. This can lead to more effective problem-solving and better outcomes for the client.

Finally, building rapport can help the consultant to stand out in a competitive marketplace. Clients are more likely to work with consultants who they feel they can trust and communicate effectively with and who they believe are genuinely interested in helping them to achieve their goals.

7.7.1   Tips for Building Rapport in Business Consulting

7.7.1.1   Do Your Research

Before you meet with a client, take the time to do your research. Learn as much as you can about the client's business, their industry, and any challenges or opportunities they are facing. This will demonstrate to the client that you are knowledgeable and interested in their business and will help to establish credibility from the outset.

7.7.1.2   Listen Carefully

One of the most important skills for building rapport is listening. When meeting with a client, be sure to give them your full attention and listen carefully to what they have to say. This will help you to understand their needs and concerns and develop a more productive working relationship.

7.7.1.3   Communicate Clearly

Effective communication is key to building rapport. Be sure to communicate clearly and concisely, and avoid using jargon or technical terms that the client may not be familiar with. This will help to ensure that the client understands your recommendations and feels confident in your abilities.

7.7.1.4   Show Empathy

Empathy is the ability to understand and share the feelings of others. In business consulting, it is important to show empathy toward the client and to understand their perspective on the challenges they are facing. This can help to build trust and create a more productive working relationship.

7.7.1.5   Be Honest and Transparent

Honesty and transparency are essential in building rapport with clients. Be upfront about any limitations or challenges that you may face in addressing their business problems, and be clear about the scope and timeframe of your engagement. This will help to establish trust and ensure that the client has realistic expectations of what you can deliver.

7.7.1.6   Demonstrate Flexibility

Flexibility is key in building rapport with clients. Be willing to adapt your approach and recommendations based on the client's needs and feedback. This will demonstrate that you are committed to their success, and can help to create a more productive working relationship.

7.7.1.7   Follow Through

Finally, it is important to follow through on your commitments. If you promise to deliver a report or complete a task by a certain deadline, make sure you do so. This will help to establish credibility and build trust with the client. Building rapport is a crucial aspect of business consulting. By establishing trust, communicating effectively, and showing empathy, consultants can create a more productive working relationship with their clients.

7.8   Effective Time Management

Effective time management is crucial for any business consulting professional. A consultant's job involves handling multiple tasks simultaneously, and time management plays a key role in ensuring all tasks are completed within deadlines. Ineffective time management can lead to missed deadlines, incomplete work, and unhappy clients. Therefore, it is important to develop strategies and habits that can help maximize productivity and manage time efficiently.

One of the most effective ways to manage time is by creating a schedule or to-do list. This allows consultants to prioritize tasks, allocate time to each task, and ensure that all tasks are completed within the given time frame. It is important to identify the tasks that are critical and need immediate attention and prioritize them accordingly. By organizing tasks in a list, consultants can keep track of their progress and ensure that all tasks are completed on time.

Another important strategy for effective time management is to minimize distractions. Distractions such as emails, social media, phone calls, and meetings can consume a significant amount of time and reduce productivity. It is important to set aside specific times for checking emails and attending meetings and to minimize interruptions during work hours. This can be achieved by turning off phone notifications, closing unnecessary tabs, and setting boundaries with colleagues.

Effective time management also involves taking breaks and managing energy levels. Working for extended periods without taking breaks can lead to burnout and decreased productivity. It is important to take breaks and engage in activities that help in recharging and refocusing, such as taking a walk, listening to music, or meditating. Managing energy levels can also involve setting boundaries between work and personal life, such as avoiding working late at night or during weekends.

Prioritizing and delegating tasks can also help manage time efficiently. Some tasks can be delegated to other team members or outsourced, freeing up time for more critical tasks. It is important to delegate tasks to the right person with the necessary skills and experience to ensure quality work.

Lastly, effective time management involves being adaptable and flexible. Unexpected events or urgent tasks may arise, and it is important to be able to adjust schedules and prioritize accordingly. By being flexible and adaptable, consultants can manage unexpected events while still ensuring that all tasks are completed on time.

Effective time management is a critical aspect of business consulting. It involves creating a schedule, minimizing distractions, taking breaks, managing energy levels, prioritizing and delegating tasks, and being adaptable and flexible. By implementing these strategies, consultants can maximize productivity and ensure that all tasks are completed within deadlines, leading to satisfied clients and successful projects.

Conclusion

The world of business consulting has been evolving rapidly, and as with many industries, it has been impacted by technology advancements and changes in client expectations. As a result, it is essential for business consultants to continually develop their skills to remain competitive in the industry. In this chapter, we will explore the future of business consulting and offer insights on how to continue developing skills in this field.

One of the most significant trends in the business consulting industry is the use of technology to improve efficiency and effectiveness. In recent years, we have seen a surge in the use of artificial intelligence and machine learning to help consultants analyze data and identify patterns that can inform their recommendations. As this technology continues to evolve, it will become even more critical for consultants to have a solid understanding of how to use these tools effectively.

Another trend we are seeing in the business consulting industry is the increasing demand for specialized expertise. As clients become more sophisticated, they are looking for consultants who have deep knowledge in specific areas, such as cybersecurity, digital transformation, or sustainability. This means that consultants must stay current on industry trends and continue to develop their expertise in their chosen areas.

To keep up with these trends, business consultants must be committed to ongoing learning and development. This can take many forms, including attending industry conferences, participating in professional development programs, or pursuing additional certifications or degrees. The key is to find opportunities that will help you stay up-to-date on the latest trends and best practices in your area of expertise.

Networking is also critical to developing your skills in the business consulting industry. By attending conferences and events, you can meet other professionals in your field and learn from their experiences. Joining professional associations or online communities can also provide opportunities to connect with other consultants and stay informed about new developments in the industry.

© The Editor(s) (if applicable) and The Author(s), under exclusive license to
Springer Nature Switzerland AG 2023
F. Addimando, *Client-Centered Business Consulting*, SpringerBriefs in
Psychology, https://doi.org/10.1007/978-3-031-42844-9

Another important aspect of developing your skills as a business consultant is working on your communication and collaboration skills. As a consultant, you will need to work closely with clients and colleagues, so it is essential to be able to communicate your ideas clearly and collaborate effectively. This may involve taking courses or workshops on topics such as presentation skills, conflict resolution, or project management.

Finally, it is critical to stay up-to-date on the latest tools and technologies that can help you be more effective in your work. Whether it's learning how to use new data analysis software or mastering the latest project management tools, staying current on these developments can help you stay competitive in the industry and provide better service to your clients.

In conclusion, the future of business consulting is both exciting and challenging. As technology continues to evolve, and client expectations continue to shift, it will be essential for consultants to remain committed to ongoing learning and development. By staying up-to-date on industry trends, networking with other professionals, and honing your communication and collaboration skills, you can position yourself for success in this dynamic field.

Further Reading

Block, Peter. 2011. *Flawless Consulting: A Guide to Getting Your Expertise Used*. Pfeiffer.
Bridges, William. 1991. *Managing Transitions: Making the Most of Change*. Nicholas Brealey Publishing.
Buzan, Tony. 1996. *The Mind Map Book: How to Use Radiant Thinking to Maximize Your Brain's Untapped Potential*. BBC Books.
Checkland, Peter. 1999. *Systems Thinking, Systems Practice*. Wiley.
Deming, W. Edwards. 2000. *The New Economics for Industry, Government, Education*. MIT Press.
Drucker, Peter. 1954. *The Practice of Management*. Harper Business.
Grant, Robert. 1991. *Cont+emporary Strategy Analysis: Concepts, Techniques, Applications*. Wiley.
Hesselbein, Frances. 2002. *The Leader of the Future 2: Visions, Strategies and Practices for the New Era*. Jossey-Bass.
Kanter, Rosabeth Moss. 1983. *The Change Masters: Innovation and Entrepreneurship in the American Corporation*. Simon & Schuster.
Lencioni, Patrick. 2010. *Getting Naked: A Business Fable About Shedding The Three Fears That Sabotage Client Loyalty*. Jossey-Bass.
Pascale, Richard Tanner. 2000. *Surfing the Edge of Chaos: The Laws of Nature and the New Laws of Business*. Crown Business.
Schein, Edgar H. 2010. *Aiutare*. Franco Angeli.
Tichy, Noel M. 2002. *The Leadership Engine: How Winning Companies Build Leaders at Every Level*. Harper Business.
Weiss, Alan. 2005. *Million Dollar Consulting: The Professional's Guide to Growing a Practice*. McGraw-Hill Education.
Womack, James P. 2007. *The Machine That Changed the World: The Story of Lean Production*. Free Press.

F. Addimando, *Client-Centered Business Consulting*, SpringerBriefs in
Psychology, https://doi.org/10.1007/978-3-031-42844-9

Index

© The Editor(s) (if applicable) and The Author(s), under exclusive license to
Springer Nature Switzerland AG 2023
F. Addimando, *Client-Centered Business Consulting*, SpringerBriefs in
Psychology, https://doi.org/10.1007/978-3-031-42844-9